Capitalism

Capitalism

The Future of an Illusion

FRED L. BLOCK

UNIVERSITY OF CALIFORNIA PRESS

University of California Press, one of the most distin-
guished university presses in the United States, enriches
lives around the world by advancing scholarship in the
humanities, social sciences, and natural sciences. Its
activities are supported by the UC Press Foundation and
by philanthropic contributions from individuals and
institutions. For more information, visit www.ucpress.edu.

University of California Press
Oakland, California

Library of Congress Cataloging-in-Publication Data

Names: Block, Fred L., author.
Title: Capitalism : the future of an illusion /
    Fred L. Block.
Description: Oakland, California : University of
    California Press, [2018] | Includes bibliographical
    references and index.
Identifiers: LCCN 2017054199 (print) | LCCN 2017059306
    (ebook) | ISBN 9780520959071 (E-book) |
    ISBN 9780520283220 (cloth : alk. paper) |
    ISBN 9780520283237 (pbk. : alk. paper)
Subjects: LCSH: Capitalism—United States. | United
    States—Economic policy. | United States—Politics
    and government. | Globalization—Economic aspects.
Classification: LCC HC103 (ebook) | LCC HC103 .B548 2018
    (print) | DDC 330.973—dc23
LC record available at https://lccn.loc.gov/2017054199

Manufactured in the United States of America

26 25 24 23 22 21 20 19 18
10 9 8 7 6 5 4 3 2 1

Contents

Acknowledgments

Some of the ideas in this book have been germinating for decades. Since these thoughts were invariably clarified and developed in dialogue, both real and imaginary, with colleagues, it follows that I have many intellectual debts. Rather than trying to identify every single individual, I will instead describe the different intellectual milieus that have shaped my thinking over the years.

The Department of Sociology at the University of California, Davis, has been a supportive home base for more than twenty-five years. Colleagues, including but not limited to Nicole Biggart, Stephanie Mudge, Sean O'Riain, Michael Peter Smith, and Vicki Smith, have had a big impact on my thinking. I have been on the editorial board of the journal *Politics & Society* since 1980, and conversations with Magali Sarfatti Larson, Molly Nolan, Erik Wright, and many others have left traces on the current book.

I have also been affiliated with the international network of Polanyi scholars coordinated by the Karl Polanyi Institute at Concordia University in Montreal. My coauthor Margaret Somers, Margie Mendell, Kari Polanyi-Levitt, Jamie Peck, and many others have pushed my thinking in new directions. The same can be said of the network of economic sociologists organized through the American Sociological Association, where I have learned much from Viviana Zelizer, Greta Krippner, Jerry Davis, and many others.

I also have benefited greatly from connections to Brazilian scholars that have been organized by Ana Celia Castro and Leonardo Burlamaqui. They also put me in conversation with European scholars such as Erik Reinert, Robert Wade, and Mariana Mazzucato. When Leonardo was a program officer at the Ford Foundation, he supported the research on innovation in the U.S. that I carried out with Matthew R. Keller, Marian Negoita, and the broader network of scholars who contributed to the edited book *State of Innovation.*

I also have debts that are closely linked to the last three years of writing this book. Two editors, Peter Richardson and Michael Aronson, responded positively to the initial proposal for this book, and this enthusiasm gave me the push to get started. Naomi Schneider has seen the work through to its conclusion. She read numerous drafts, sometimes with remarkable speed, and has repeatedly offered sage advice. Sue Carter did an outstanding job copyediting the manuscript.

At critical points, feedback from reviewers and close friends has improved the book greatly. Specifically, Peter Evans, Karl Klare, Greta Krippner, Magali Sarfatti Larson, Frances Fox Piven, Michael Peter Smith, Margaret Somers, and Jay Varellas provided many important criticisms. They are, however, absolved from responsibility from the remaining shortcomings of this book.

Finally, I am deeply grateful to the continuing love and support of my wife, Carole, and my daughters, Miriam and Jude.

May 1, 2017

CHAPTER ONE

The Capitalist Illusion

"The Economy, Stupid," read the famous sign that James Carville posted in Bill Clinton's Little Rock campaign headquarters in the 1992 presidential race. It was a reminder to the campaign team that they needed to focus on the weakness of the economic recovery under their opponent, President George H. W. Bush. Both before that election and certainly since, many presidential campaigns have been decided by voters' perceptions of the strength or weakness of the economy. Donald Trump's surprising victory in 2016 had much to do with a large segment of the electorate believing that the economy under Obama had failed to generate the kind of growth that they expected. Even some voters who were willing to credit President Obama with rescuing the economy from free fall at the time of his inauguration were worried that Hillary Clinton was unlikely to do well in generating good jobs and increasing real wages. A lot of voters believed that Donald Trump's business success would make him a more effective economic manager than his opponent.

While views about the health of the economy really matter for politics, so also do beliefs about what kind of economy we have, how it works, and what policies might strengthen or weaken it. Today, virtually everybody—left, right, and center—believes both that our economy is capitalist and that the economy is autonomous, coherent, and regulated by its own internal logics. Many go to the next step and embrace the idea that if we pursue policies that conflict with the imperatives of capitalism, they will inevitably backfire and produce slower growth and fewer jobs.

Here is the problem. For years now, voters have cast their ballots for the candidate they think will manage the economy more effectively, but they are almost always disappointed by the results. Disappointment occurs because presidents and their advisers believe that because we have a capitalist economy, our policy options are extremely constrained. Whatever ambitions a newly elected president has when he first arrives at 1600 Pennsylvania Avenue, he pretty soon discovers that there is no set of legitimate policy tools that can deliver what the public wants because of the constraints of capitalism.

And so our politics have been caught in a loop that alternates between center-left Democrats and increasingly extreme Republicans, none of whom have been able to make good on their economic promises. Meanwhile, much of the electorate remains convinced that the nation is headed in the wrong direction. It now seems inevitable that a disappointed public will turn against whoever is in the White House; the only question is how soon that disillusionment will set in.

There is, however, a way out of this cycle of raised hopes followed by disappointment, and it involves challenging the received wisdom that capitalism operates according to its own inner laws. My title, *Capitalism: The Future of an Illusion*, is borrowed from Sigmund Freud's 1927 *The Future of an Illusion.* The illusion that Freud was challenging was religion; he argued in that book that religions tell made-up stories that address some of the primal psychological conflicts of human existence. At the time, Freud's title offended many, but today, it is far more radical and disturbing to suggest that capitalism is an illusion. After all, profit-oriented firms own and control most of the world's productive capacity. Why would anybody suggest that a label that is so obviously appropriate is, instead, an illusion?

Here, Freud is a useful guide. In describing religion as an illusion, Freud did not imagine that it was inconsequential or unimportant. He knew that people's religious beliefs shaped their actions; he wrote his book shortly after World War I, when millions had died at the front imagining that they were fighting with God on their side. Moreover, Freud was keenly aware that religious teachings were linked to puritanical attitudes toward human sexuality that he viewed as psychologically destructive. In a word, Freud was insisting that religion was both extremely important and an illusion.

My argument is parallel to this. The widespread belief that we live in a capitalist society is enormously consequential. But many of the stories that people tell us about the nature of capitalism are myths comparable to the biblical story of the Garden of Eden. The project of this book is to debunk the view of capitalism that has become hegemonic. Dispelling this illusion will open up possibilities for political and economic reform that exist now only on the margins of contemporary political debate.[1]

Deep political crises in both the U.S. and Europe indicate the urgency of opening up space for major reforms. Trump's unprecedented election is a symptom of how badly the U.S. political system is broken. It is the first time since 1940 that a political out-sider was able to win the nomination of one of the major parties, but Trump is a far more troubling outsider than Wendell Willkie. Trump won his party's nomination because a majority of Repub-lican voters were in open revolt against the party establishment. His populist rhetoric against immigrants and free trade deals and his promise to "make America great again" resonated with voters. During the same primary season, Bernie Sanders's populist chal-lenge to Hillary Clinton was also far more successful than most observers had expected. Even though Clinton ultimately pre-vailed, the resonance of Sanders's attacks on the millionaire and billionaire class also indicated deep currents of discontent among voters.

John Judis has recently linked the populist insurgencies led by Trump and Sanders to similar patterns in European politics.[2] Because of the differences in the electoral systems, the European challengers tend to come from outsider parties, but Judis shows that populist parties of the right and of the left have been gaining support in many countries of Europe, while support for the tra-ditional mainstream governing parties has been eroding. The right-wing populist parties include the United Kingdom Inde-pendence Party, the French National Front, the Danish People's Party, and the Alternative Party in Germany, while the left-wing populist parties include Syriza in Greece and Podemos in Spain. Judis and other observers argue that the recent successes of these populist insurgencies are due to the economic difficulties that the U.S. and Europe have experienced since the global financial crisis of 2008. Mainstream parties have insisted for years that a global economy based on free trade and free capital mobility would lift all boats and assure ever-rising standards of living. Yet the public sees instead rising levels of unemployment and underemployment, stagnant incomes, and greater economic uncertainty. Their votes for these various populist insurgencies are a signal to the leaders of the establishment that something is very wrong and that something must be done.

But the messages of these protest voters are not getting through. In Greece in 2015, an angry electorate put Syriza, a newly formed leftist populist party, in charge of the government. But in negotiating a new financial aid package for Greece, the leaders of the European Community told the new government that it had to ignore the voters. The European leadership insisted that Greece continue the same cruel austerity measures that had led the electorate to revolt in the first place.

To be sure, Greece is an extreme case. But for years now, highly respected economists have been saying that in both Europe and the U.S., governments should take advantage of historically low long-term interest rates to make major investments in new infrastructure spending as a way to revive these weak economies. Big government investments in infrastructure would put some people to work, might stimulate greater private investment, and could assist the fight to ameliorate the ravages of climate change. And yet this increased infrastructure spending has not happened. Centrist, center-right, and hard-right political leaders have worked together to block increased infrastructure spending.

How do we explain this? When voters everywhere are turning to populist protest candidates, the job of mainstream politicians is to do something to reduce voter discontent. That is certainly what happened in the United States in the 1930s. When faced with a threat from socialist and communist movements on the left and populists such as Huey Long and Father Coughlin on the right, Franklin Roosevelt and congressional Democrats carried out the ambitious legislative reforms of the New Deal.[3]

And in the period right after World War II, centrist politicians in Europe threatened by strong left-wing movements carried out sweeping reforms that included a significant expansion of the state's role both in managing the economy and in providing various forms of social insurance.[4] However, this most recent period of populist agitation has produced no comparable experimentation with bold reforms.

One would think that there would at least be extensive debate and discussion of major reform measures that might restore economic prosperity. But that has not happened. Aside from some discussion about more spending on infrastructure, there have been very few bold ideas to revitalize the European Community or accelerate growth in the U.S. economy. And despite his election rhetoric, once in office, Trump has simply followed the familiar Republican agenda of steep tax cuts for corporations and the rich. At the very least, one might expect that the parties that are out of power would be debating these kinds of reform ideas in the hope that voters would turn to them in the next election, rather than to the protest parties, but such new thinking is largely absent on both sides of the Atlantic.

One standard explanation for this policy inertia is that mainstream politicians in all of these countries have become so tightly intertwined with entrenched business interests that they are unwilling to entertain any ideas that might threaten those powerful economic elites. But business interests are not highly unified; many business leaders are also unhappy with the poor performance of the global economy in recent years. Many large firms, for example, would benefit enormously from greatly increased public-sector infrastructure investments. In fact, even in the U.S., there are signs of business interests lobbying for such expenditures.[5] In earlier reform epochs when political leaders were pressured by populist revolts, they found ways to shape a reform agenda that business leaders could live with.

But it is not so easy to dismiss the role of far-right business interests in the U.S., such as the extremely wealthy Koch brothers.[6] They have organized right-wing billionaires and millionaires who espouse an extreme anti-state ideology. Through campaign funding and think tanks, this group has gained extraordinary influence over the Republican congressional delegations, and they have been able to block even relatively modest reform ideas that violate their "small state" beliefs. However, this does not explain the caution of the Democratic Party establishment, and Europe by and large does not have groups analogous to the Koch brothers' network.

A more persuasive argument focuses on the specific influence of one sector of the business community—the financial sector, which has grown enormously over the last thirty years.[7] Bankers have long been the upholders of economic orthodoxy; they almost always oppose deficit spending by governments and any significant changes to the status quo. Moreover, we have seen recent examples of center-left governments that were strongly supportive of financial interests. Bill Clinton's administration (1993–2000) and Tony Blair's New Labour government in England were notorious for their solicitous approach to financial firms on Wall Street and in the City of London.

In tracing out the linkages between financial interests and establishment politicians, the most useful idea is that of "cognitive capture."[8] It is not just personal connections and campaign contributions that make political leaders beholden to financial interests. The core problem is that most politicians, including "populists" such as Trump, have adopted the same beliefs about how the economy works as the financial community. It is as though they all went to school together and read the same books, so they share the same belief system. This means that bold reforms of the existing system are automatically ruled out as irrational and counterproductive.

But what are the actual ideas that have cognitively captured the minds of these political leaders? This is precisely what I am calling the capitalist illusion. Both elites and the wider public have come to believe that given the nature of capitalism, all that can be done to stimulate growth is to balance government budgets, cut regulations, and rely on central banks to expand the money supply. Any more radical reforms are rejected in advance because they are allegedly incompatible with the nature of capitalism.

This cognitive capture occurs because of the formidable power of finance, direct linkages between politicians and wealthy donors in the financial sector, and a decades-long campaign to convince everyone that capitalism is an internally coherent and unchangeable system. In short, political elites have been extraordinarily passive in the face of growing populist discontent precisely because they are in thrall to these capitalist illusions, which rule out consideration of reforms that could potentially revitalize weakening economies.

Reversing this cognitive capture could not be more urgent. As long as political and business elites imagine that they are powerless because capitalism cannot be changed, we face a replay of the 1930s, with dangerous authoritarians seizing power and unleashing the threat of another world war.[9] But this danger can be averted if large segments of the public and some of these elites are able to recognize our collective ability to carry out bold reforms that could, once again, produce an economy that meets the needs of the citizenry. This is the argument of the present book.

Since cognitive capture looms so large, the focus of this book is on the definition of capitalism that prevails on the center and the right of the political spectrum. But the story is complicated because the term "capitalism" was basically invented and popularized by the socialist left. However, key aspects of that leftist definition have been appropriated by mainstream thinkers. So, for example, the idea that capitalism cannot be effectively reformed was central to the writings of Karl Marx, Friedrich Engels, and many later Marxists. They insisted that the only way to overcome the evils of the existing order was to replace it with something radically different—socialism. Now, however, it is writers on the center and the right who argue that we have to accept the negative aspects of the current system precisely because the only real alternative is socialism, which, they insist, would mean accepting a much diminished standard of living.

As I seek to debunk the capitalist illusion, it would be too confusing to weave in the story of the complex ways in which thinkers on the left and on the right have influenced each other's formulations. Instead, my plan is to concentrate on criticizing the understanding of capitalism that prevails among thinkers in the center and on the right. In the afterword, I address some of the illusions about the nature of capitalism that are held by some on the political left.

THE NATURE OF THE CAPITALIST ILLUSION

When I describe the capitalist illusion and its principal components, they will not all be immediately recognizable. These are not the kinds of claims that one puts on bumper stickers or that candidates shout out on the campaign stump. They are, rather, like the hidden part of the iceberg that lies submerged and invisible under the water's surface. They are the unstated assumptions and beliefs that are necessary to support the familiar rhetoric about economic policy that dominates our political debates. It is precisely because they are not readily visible that it takes a whole book to identify and challenge these illusions.

The core illusion is the idea that capitalism is a system that has its own logic and rules that must be obeyed or we risk losing the material well-being that has been achieved to date. It is also believed that this system has been largely stable for at least two hundred years. Most definitions of capitalism are explicit in defining it as a system in which owners of private property compete on markets to make profits, with the consequence that firms have strong incentives to become ever more efficient. But this now hegemonic understanding of capitalism includes four implicit corollaries that are responsible for the illusion of unity, coherence, and permanence.

It is important to emphasize here that many recent books and articles define the nature of capitalism in ways that are very different from the capitalist illusion that I am describing here.[10] Sometimes these definitions of capitalism are quite lengthy, as these thinkers seek to differentiate their view from the simplicity of the illusionary view that capitalism is unified and coherent. But these efforts run up against the problem that the meaning of familiar words will sometimes change through usage. This is something that parents of teenagers sometimes recognize with horror. For example, the word "dating" that they associate with two people chastely enjoying dinner and a movie now often refers to a sexual relationship. Whether the word is "capitalism" or "dating," it is a futile endeavor to try to restore the older definition.

The first corollary in this now dominant definition of capitalism is that the economy is and should be autonomous, so that it can follow its own logic. It is recognized that government must do certain things, including enforcing laws of property and contract and providing for national defense, but government must avoid acting in ways that interfere with the autonomy of the economy. The second corollary is that there is a fundamental tension between democracy and capitalism because the voters might foolishly elect leaders who interfere with the autonomy of the market by raising taxes too much or imposing burdensome regulations. The third corollary is that capitalism requires individuals to be responsive to the signals of the marketplace, so society must emphasize the value of individuals pursuing their economic self-interest, including, particularly, the accumulation of wealth. The final corollary is a theory of causality that argues that capitalism works because it has the proper micro-foundations. This means that individuals are motivated to pursue their self-interest within a set of property relations that assures the appropriate rewards to those who make productive investments.

Together, the definition and these four corollaries constitute a kind of social theory about capitalist societies. But it is different from most other social theories because it is unapologetically a form of economic determinism.[11] The social theory of capitalism that I am describing has a logic similar to that of Carville's 1992 sign: it is the economy that drives and shapes society, and we must do whatever it takes to make sure that the basic mechanisms of capitalism are not impeded.

This embrace of economic determinism is somewhat surprising because for many decades the political valence of such doctrines was very different. Thinkers of the left, especially Marxists, were denounced for having a view of the world that rested on economic determinism. Conservatives claimed that attributing all that causal power to the economy neglected the importance in social life of politics, religion, and ideas. More than a century ago, when Charles Beard advanced his economic theory of the U.S. Constitution, it was considered a scandal because he replaced all of the passion and vision of the Founders with a story that centered on groups defending their economic interests.[12] Even half a century ago, when I was in college, liberal professors expressed discomfort with the New Left–inspired economic determinism that ran through the essays and papers I wrote for my classes.

But all of this has changed; many on the center and the right and some on the left now proudly adhere to the capitalist social theory that I have described. And the fact that it builds in economic determinism has not interfered with its popularity. On the contrary, the last three decades, during which time this social theory became dominant, have also seen the diminishing influence of competing social theories that reject economic determinism. Sociology, particularly, has lost much of its influence on public debates. In the 1950s, work by social thinkers such as David Riesman and C. Wright Mills reached a broad audience. In the 1970, the sociologist Daniel Bell was among the society's most influential intellectuals.[13] Today, however, very few social thinkers are known outside of their discipline, and their books never make it anywhere near the best-seller list.[14] The capitalist social theory has taken over public debate.

This theory, as well as each of its main components, however, is incorrect. The fundamental reality is that capitalism, whether conceptualized in global or national terms, is not a coherent and unified system. On the contrary, successful market economies depend on a complex combination of conflicting institutions and motivations; they are contradictory and unstable, and they periodically require major structural reorganizations. During these reform epochs, nobody has a roadmap or a guidebook;

experimentation—sometimes bold experimentation—has been required for societies to identify the reforms needed to pave the way for economic revitalization.[15]

Again, I am not alone in challenging this capitalist social theory. A large body of work by social scientists has by now shown many of the ways in which this framework is wrong. For example, many political scientists and sociologists have contributed to a literature on "varieties of capitalism" that shows large and durable differences in the institutional arrangements of nations with capitalist property relations.[16] If, for example, the U.S. and Germany have very different systems of labor relations, very different welfare systems, and very different financial systems, it logically follows that capitalism is not one coherent unified thing.

But while these analysts have correctly emphasized how much variation and variability there is within different profit-oriented economies, their message has been drowned out by the hegemonic view that capitalism is a unified and largely unchanging system. When they stress the variations within capitalist societies, their audience tends to focus on the commonalities. This is because when most people see or hear the word "capitalism," it brings to mind the whole capitalist social theory that I am describing, and this occurs whether people have positive or negative views of capitalism. In fact, during the campaign of Bernie Sanders for the Democratic nomination, public opinion polls showed astonishing numbers of young people in the U.S. who said they preferred socialism to capitalism.[17] But whether they hate it or like it, they conceptualize capitalism as a unified, coherent, and unchanging system whose inner logic must be obeyed.

Scholars or pundits who try to give the term "capitalism" a different meaning than that inhering in the capitalist illusion are in the awkward situation that Lewis Carroll described in

Through the Looking Glass.[18] Alice has an illuminating conversation with Humpty Dumpty that is very much about the nature of words and concepts. It begins with Humpty pointing out the superiority of celebrating unbirthdays over birthdays, since there are 364 of the former and only one of the latter:

> "And only *one* for birthday presents, you know. There's glory for you!"
>
> "I don't know what you mean by 'glory,'" Alice said.
>
> Humpty Dumpty smiled contemptuously. "Of course you don't—till I tell you. I meant 'there's a nice knock-down argument for you!'"
>
> "But 'glory' doesn't mean 'a nice knock-down argument,'" Alice objected.
>
> "When *I* use a word," Humpty Dumpty said, in rather a scornful tone, "it means just what I choose it to mean—neither more nor less."
>
> "The question is," said Alice, "whether you can make words mean so many different things."
>
> "The question is," said Humpty Dumpty, "which is to be master—that's all."

Lewis Carroll's point is that since language is socially created, we cannot exercise the kind of dominion over words that Humpty imagines. Words not only have definitions, but also associations and connotations. And some words in particular, such as "capitalism" or "socialism" or "liberalism," which have been central to political debates for extended periods of time, carry with them an enormous weight of associations. When social scientists attempt to give one of these words a precise definition, they are being like Humpty Dumpty—imagining that they can exercise dominion over words that have acquired a life and a set of meanings of their own. The reality is that whatever the definition, when the reader sees the word "capitalism," he or she is likely to plug in the meaning that has been acquired through previous experiences and learning. And sometimes, the meanings that the reader inserts are exactly the opposite of what was intended.

THE ORIGINS OF THE ILLUSION

So where did this illusion come from and how did it become so dominant in shaping the views of both elites and publics? It was actually only in the 1980s that the word "capitalism" came into wide usage in the U.S. During the Cold War, the term was generally avoided in polite discourse because it was closely associated with Soviet and Communist Chinese anti-U.S. propaganda. When I was a college student, the term was still strongly associated with old left groups such as the Communist Party.

However, in 1965, Paul Potter, then president of Students for a Democratic Society (SDS), gave a speech at the first big student-led anti–Vietnam War march in Washington, D.C. The thrust of the speech was that the Vietnam War was not an accident, but the logical outcome of an entire system. The crux of the speech went as follows:

> What kind of system is it that allows good men to make those kinds of decisions? What kind of system is it that justifies the United States or any country seizing the destinies of the Vietnamese people and using them callously for its own purpose? What kind of system is it that disenfranchises people in the South, leaves millions upon millions of people throughout the country impoverished and excluded from the mainstream and promise of American society, that creates faceless and terrible bureaucracies and makes those the place where people spend their lives and do their work, that consistently puts material values before human values and still persists in calling itself free and still persists in finding itself fit to police the

world? What place is there for ordinary men in that system and how are they to control it, make it bend itself to their wills rather than bending them to its?

We must name that system. We must name it, describe it, analyze it, understand it and change it. For it is only when that system is changed and brought under control that there can be any hope for stopping the forces that create a war in Vietnam today or a murder in the South tomorrow or all the incalculable, innumerable more subtle atrocities that are worked on people all over—all the time.[19]

I was a college freshman then, and I was in the crowd listening to this speech. I can remember the excitement we felt when he uttered the imperative to name the system. We all knew that he was talking about capitalism, but the term was still so forbidden that Potter did not actually use the word. We shared his conviction that racial inequality and the Vietnam War were proof that the basic economic structures of U.S. society needed to be challenged and changed.

The irony is that since that speech, the term "capitalism" moved from the margins to the center of political discourse in the United States. Some of the credit for this change can be taken by the New Left of the 1960s and the accomplishments of scholars who were part of a revival of the Marxist tradition in universities in the 1960s and 1970s.[20] In the 1970s, Immanuel Wallerstein, for example, published the first volume of a history of the modern capitalist world system, and several radical economists published a popular text called *The Capitalist System.*[21] These efforts helped give the term "capitalism" greater intellectual legitimacy; it was no longer just a tool of Soviet propaganda. Yet the influence of these leftist intellectuals on the political mainstream was short-lived because the country lurched rightward in the 1980s with the election of Ronald Reagan.

The heavy lifting in making the term "capitalism" respectable was actually done by a small group of right-wing intellectuals. As early as 1962, Milton Friedman published his conservative manifesto *Capitalism and Freedom*, and four years later the libertarian thinker Ayn Rand published a book of essays called *Capitalism: The Unknown Ideal*.[22] Both Friedman and Rand were hoping to flip the term—to strip it of its negative associations in much the same way as the Black Power movement proudly embraced the word "black," which had earlier conveyed stigma. But the term "capitalism" was still so unpopular that using it just confirmed that Friedman and Rand were marginal intellectual figures. However, other conservatives eventually joined them, and the effort to flip the term's political valance ultimately succeeded. Malcolm Forbes, publisher of *Forbes Magazine*, adopted the slogan "Forbes—Capitalist Tool" in 1966.[23] Denouncing a politician as a "capitalist tool" had long been one of the most stinging insults in the repertoire of leftist parties. Just as African American demonstrators might chant "I'm black and I'm proud," so Forbes wanted businesspeople to say that they were capitalist and proud.

But the most important work along these lines was done by the neoconservative intellectual and publicist Irving Kristol. His *Two Cheers for Capitalism*, published in 1978, acknowledged that the term "capitalism" had historically belonged to opponents of the system, but Kristol argued that conservative defenders of the status quo would gain power by embracing the term.[24] Kristol was thoroughly familiar with Marxism; he had been one of those famously argumentative Trotskyists in Alcove 1 in the City College cafeteria in the 1930s. He recognized that one key advantage of "capitalism" as a term was its focus on the systemic consequences of certain fundamental arrangements. Marx had argued that a capitalist does not seek to pursue profits because he or she is greedy or suffers some character defect. The individual capitalist does not have any choice; the failure to pursue profits will quickly end his or her business career. The relentless pursuit of profit is a structural imperative of the entire system.

The conservative writer George Gilder quickly followed up on Kristol's lead in his 1981 book *Wealth and Poverty*, which became one of the bibles of the Reagan era.[25] While Kristol had been unwilling to give capitalism a third cheer, Gilder had no such hesitation. He embraced capitalism as superior to all other economic systems on the grounds of both efficiency and morality. He portrayed capitalists as heroic moral figures who selflessly served the interests of society as a whole by their willingness to make risky investments. On this basis, Gilder argued for massive tax cuts that would reward the wealthy as well as the dismantling of many of the regulations that constrained business firms. Gilder's book was hugely influential and sold more than a million copies.

Gilder and these other conservative intellectuals understood that appropriating the idea of capitalism as a unified and coherent system had the potential to give the right greatly increased leverage in its struggles against political liberalism. Historically, conservative thinkers had emphasized the voluntary and individualistic dimension of free market arrangements. They had defined a market economy as the aggregation of contracts entered into by separate individuals, and they had gone on to argue that it is desirable for both liberty and economic efficiency to allow these voluntary arrangements to operate with a minimum of "outside interference"—especially from government. But this formulation had been weakened by decades of arguments by political and legal reformers that changes in the legal rules and regulations governing private transactions were consistent with the principle of voluntary contracting.

In fact, many of the reforms carried out by Franklin Roosevelt's New Deal were justified in the legal arena as being consistent with voluntary contracting.[26] So, for example, a series of reforms of the rules governing the labor market gave employees a variety of protections against overly long hours, inadequate wages, and management's refusal to engage in collective bargaining. But these arguments were justified by insisting that the new rules merely modified the context in which employee and employer negotiated their voluntary contracts. After all, the goal of collective bargaining was for the two sides to negotiate a mutually agreeable contract.

In the 1960s and 1970s, as consumer and environmental consciousness was growing in the U.S., this kind of incremental reform process gained new momentum. Even after Republicans gained the White House in 1969, Richard Nixon signed into law legislation creating new government agencies to protect the environment and improve occupational health and safety. Once again, proponents argued that the new rules just modified the context in which contracts were negotiated. However, businesses felt that they were facing an ever-stricter regulatory environment where their freedom to make profits was being severely constrained.

This is why Kristol's project of stealing the concept of capitalism was so important for business interests. The voluntary contracting framework no longer provided protection from the incremental expansion of new rules and regulations. The logic was unassailable. If we have rules that block business from selling certain dangerous products, why not extend those laws to cover unsafe automobiles or toys that could hurt children? There were no broad theoretical grounds for stopping this incremental expansion of regulation. But if one argues that all of the individual choices that are made in the market aggregate into a coherent and cohesive system, then one is in a much stronger position to resist incremental reforms. Systems demand obedience to their organizing imperatives, and measures that are inconsistent with those imperatives can be expected to produce predictably damaging consequences. Newton's third law of motion—for every action, there is an equal and opposite reaction—describes the characteristics of a system. It follows that going against the logic of the system will inevitably produce equal and opposite undesirable consequences.

In a word, Irving Kristol and other conservative intellectuals and strategists did to Marx what Marx said he had done to Hegel—stood him on his head. Marx had emphasized the systemic character of capitalism as a way to demonstrate the futility of reform proposals. He and Engels wanted radical transformation—a "root and branch" change in the form of economic organization—and their analyses and political initiatives were designed to persuade others that only a revolutionary challenge to capitalism could succeed in transforming it.[27]

But by the time of Kristol's intervention, revolution was no longer a serious danger to existing market arrangements in the U.S. Kristol and his conservative allies were far more worried that the United States would follow the path of European social democracies, which had an elaborate regulatory structure and extensive public provision of social services. So they eagerly appropriated Marx's analysis to show the profound dangers of any effort to reform the "capitalist system." In 1965, Paul Potter had urged his listeners to name the system. But once the society's intellectuals and elites had named, described, and analyzed the system as capitalism, reformist efforts were placed at a tremendous disadvantage. In fact, under conservative hegemony, many of the incremental reforms that had been won between the 1930s and the 1970s were successfully dismantled with the justification that giving businesses greater leeway would make capitalism work better.

THE ROLE OF ECONOMICS AND ECONOMIC POPULARIZATIONS

While Irving Kristol deserves a lot of credit for popularizing the capitalist illusion, his ultimate success depended on parallel developments in the discipline of economics that were later broadly diffused to the public. As noted, Milton Friedman used the word "capitalism" in a book title as early as 1962. Friedman was one of the first to recognize that redefining markets as a unified and coherent capitalist system would empower advocates of the free market and weaken their liberal opponents.

From the 1950s onward, Friedman and his Chicago colleagues were engaged in a war against the dominant Keynesian faction within the U.S. economics discipline. The Keynesians, followers of John Maynard Keynes, developed their views in response to the Great Depression of the 1930s. They believed that government should take an active role in moving the economy toward full employment and correcting other market failures. Friedman and his colleagues insisted that if markets were allowed to be self-regulating, they would achieve optimal results, and they insisted that government actions almost always produced perverse and undesirable consequences.[28]

Friedman and his allies were provided an opportunity by the economic difficulties that the U.S. economy experienced in the 1970s. A period of stagflation that combined slow economic growth with persistent inflationary pressures was an embarrassment for the reigning Keynesian faction. The economy was supposed to have elevated unemployment or elevated inflation, but not both at the same time. Friedman's faction triumphed within the discipline; thus began an extended period during which mainstream economists became more enthusiastic about markets and considerably less enthusiastic about governmental policies.

One of the main weapons that the Friedmanites used in their battle to discredit and replace the dominant Keynesian faction was the insistence that their opponents' work was not built on solid micro-foundations. By this they meant that the Keynesian theory of how the economy worked was not sufficiently connected to accounts of how individual economic actors responded to market signals. For the Friedmanites, any convincing argument had to start with rational economic actors making particular choices. This proved to be an effective weapon against the Keynesians, but as we shall see later, this insistence on a theory of causality centering on individual choices results in a social theory that is blind to the exercise of power in the modern world.

The Friedmanite triumph over the Keynesians legitimated the rise of financial economics, and the successes of that field made possible the spectacular growth of financial markets. The Keynesians had a healthy skepticism about finance because they remembered the speculative stock market boom of the late 1920s that resulted in the 1929 crash and the subsequent depression. But the growing legitimacy of the Chicago School made it possible for a new generation of financial economists to argue that the new tools that they were developing could greatly increase the efficiency with which capital is allocated to different purposes, and this would mean greater prosperity for all.

With Ronald Reagan's election as president in 1980, these ideas were put into action. New regulations allowed for the trading of previously unknown financial products, and changes in the tax law made such trading a more lucrative activity. At the same time, legislative changes opened up much greater opportunities for individuals to save for their own retirement through tax-deferred accounts. The consequence was a fantastic increase in the size of the financial sector of the economy that contributed to the severity of the crisis in 2008.[29] Almost overnight, a new strata of super-rich individuals appeared, including Wall Street traders, dealmakers at investment banks, and private equity and hedge fund managers, some of whom were able to make tens or hundreds of millions of dollars in a given year.

One of the most important aspects of this financialization of the economy has been the diffusion of the concept of capitalism elaborated by Friedman, Kristol, and Gilder. Some of the popularizers were the writers of fabulously successful business books that explained how people could get rich in this exciting new economy. Others were the financial advisors and financial writers who explained to the middle and upper class how they needed to invest their savings, taking advantage of new opportunities in the financial markets. Still others were the thinkers and policy analysts, whose numbers expanded dramatically as a whole group of right-wing think tanks and policy organizations expanded from the mid-1970s onward. Finally, many politicians incorporated the new understanding of capitalism into their standard speeches.[30]

To be sure, these popularizers did not explain the nature of capitalism systematically or even explicitly. But their impact over time was to convey to the public the idea that capitalism is a unified, coherent, and unchanging system whose inner laws must be obeyed. With versions of this story line repeated day after day by armies of popularizers over more than thirty years, this view of capitalism has been burned into the consciousness of both elites and publics.

THE PLAN

My argument is that the capitalist illusion is an entire economistic social theory that has become part of society's common sense. But this erroneous theory distorts our perceptions and ties us up in political knots, making it far more difficult to see what kinds of changes in institutions at the local, national, and global level could help us to address the multiple crises that we face. However, one cannot effectively challenge such a theory without offering a compelling alternative theory. We need theories to make sense of the world, and even when we see that a particular theory has big weaknesses, we are reluctant to discard it until we have found an alternative.

The alternative theory I propose relies heavily on four somewhat distinct strands of scholarship. The first includes the works of a number of heterodox economic thinkers that includes Karl Polanyi, Albert Hirschman, and J.K. Gibson-Graham, all of whom have advanced powerful critiques of the economy as a self-regulating mechanism.[31] The second is the work of legal scholars—both those of the 1930s and 1940s, including legal realists such as Robert Hale, and more recent critical scholars such as Duncan Kennedy, Karl Klare, and Roberto Unger.[32] All of these thinkers have helped to deconstruct economic categories and have challenged what Unger calls the "false necessity" of standard economic rhetorics. The third is the work of contemporary economic sociologists, a number of whom work in an explicitly Polanyian tradition. These include Peter Evans, Greta Krippner, Margaret Somers, and Viviana Zelizer.[33] Finally, there are the postindustrial theorists: Daniel Bell (who taught me when I was an undergraduate), Larry Hirschhorn (we wrote together decades ago), and the late historian Martin J. Sklar.[34] To be sure, many of these people might well disagree with how I have used their ideas to fit my framework. But they have constructed the foundation on which I have tried to build.

In proposing this alternative social theory, I confront a fairly common dilemma of exposition. The first option is to lay out the alternative framework from the start and then show how it explains things better than the dominant view. The other is to develop the alternative in the process of showing the limitations of the prevailing framework. Both of these choices have significant downsides, however. Laying out an alternative framework by starting with first principles is usually a tedious process that can strike readers as abstract and unpersuasive. Yet developing the alternative as one criticizes the dominant framework is often confusing. When a reader doesn't know where the author is headed, it can be difficult to follow the argument through the process of demolition.

My plan is to pursue a hybrid strategy that combines elements of the two approaches. In the next chapter, I will put my cards on the table, as it were, and explain in fairly concise terms the basic premises of my conceptual approach. While this is not a full elaboration of my framework, it should be enough for the reader to make sense of the alternative that I am offering. The next four chapters will focus on critique, showing what is wrong with the dominant and familiar way of thinking. In the conclusion, I will show how when we embrace the alternative I have proposed, we open up political possibilities rendered invisible by dominant modes of thought. Finally, in the afterword, I clarify how my perspective differs from views that continue to be voiced on the political left.

The way I develop my critique of existing ways of thinking follows standard practices in the social sciences. Books or articles often begin by saying that the literature in the field has explained a particular phenomenon in terms of theory A or theory B or theory C. The author then provides data to show that all of these theories are inadequate and only theory D provides an elegant and powerful way to make sense of the fact patterns.

This is the model that I am following. Given the complexity, there is no choice but to piece together strands of data from many different sources to construct an argument. This is what historians and other social scientists who study large-scale social change have done for many years. It is, for example, what Max Weber did in his multiple studies designed to explain why "rational capitalism" achieved its breakthrough in Western Europe rather than in other parts of the world. Hence, I will be drawing on aggregate data that reports trends over time in employment, economic output, and patterns of residential settlement, as well as a wide variety of more focused studies, journalistic reports, analyses of trends in academic literature, and my own observations over the last fifty years.

In the next chapter, I contrast the capitalist social theory with my alternative social theory. The capitalist social theory views the economy as similar to a natural entity—a living creature or a planetary system—that obeys a distinct set of laws. My alternative approach uses the metaphor of construction: a market economy, even a profit-oriented economy, is built out of many different kinds of materials and does not have its own distinct set of laws. Moreover, it is constantly in the process of changing and being reconstructed. In explaining why it is wrong to naturalize the economy or see it as similar to an organism, I directly challenge the first corollary of the capitalist social theory: that the economy is and should be autonomous.

In chapter 3, I take on the second corollary—the idea that there is a fundamental tension between a profit-oriented economy and democracy. I argue that democracy and democratic practices are part of what has made a profit-oriented economy work effectively, and that trying to shield the economy from the decisions of voters has economically disastrous consequences. In chapter 4, I look at the third corollary—the claim that the economy works best when people pursue their economic self-interest single-mindedly. I show that, in fact, the celebration of unlimited wealth is bad for both the economy and the society.

Chapter 5 takes on the mistaken belief that the core institutional structures of capitalism have remained unchanged for centuries; it argues that there have been continuous and dramatic shifts in the way that economic activity is organized. Chapter 6 challenges the fourth corollary—the theory of causality that imagines that the basic structures of a capitalist society are built up from the micro-foundations of individual choices. Here I return to the construction metaphor and argue that the way the economy is built has an enormous influence on the choices that individuals make. The structures of the economy can be rebuilt, I argue, in ways that provide individuals with much broader choices and the capability of building a better and more resilient society. In chapter 7, I pull the argument together by suggesting some of the possibilities that are open to us once we overcome the capitalist illusion.

CHAPTER TWO

Elaborating an Alternative

The word "capitalism" now suggests an entire social theory that sees the market economy as being autonomous, coherent, and regulated by its own internal logics. It is often seen as similar to an organism that has its own particular DNA. My alternative is to think of a market economy as similar to a building that is periodically remodeled for new uses and new circumstances. Think, for example, of Downton Abbey—the location for the television drama. The building that was used as the set, Highclere Castle, dates to the seventeenth century. However, it has been repeatedly added to and renovated over the years, with major changes in the infrastructure for plumbing, heating, and electricity. In these remodeling projects, the contractors maintained the building's structural integrity, but they did not think that the building had its own internal laws that had to be obeyed.

The possibilities for repurposing the internal space of such a building are almost unlimited. Even if the original structure was intended to visually represent the magnificence of the landed aristocracy, it would not be difficult to reorganize the facility to serve as the headquarters for a high-tech firm in which software engineers had easy access to top executives. The metaphor is meant to suggest that within the parameters of an economy with private ownership and the pursuit of profitability, there is still very wide leeway to decide how large or small a role the state will play, how much inequality will be tolerated, and how deep and broad democratic governance will be.

But these possibilities for reconstruction have been made invisible to us because of the capitalist social theory. The misrecognition operates at several distinct levels. First, the way that we think about market transactions is fundamentally wrong; we think of them as spontaneous interactions rather than as carefully choreographed productions. Second, when we aggregate those market transactions into a national economy, we think of it as an autonomous entity that follows its own logic and rules. Third, we similarly conceptualize the global economy as an autonomous, self-regulating entity rather than understanding it as something that has been carefully constructed and reconstructed over time. Finally, the capitalist social theory is basically indifferent to what an economy is actually producing at any given time; the logic and relations are the same whether the dominant product is wool or steel or computer chips. However, in the alternative proposed here, changes in production have huge consequences for the structure and organization of a society.

THE LOGIC OF THE MARKET

It is pretty much axiomatic to think of a market as an arena dominated by the pursuit of self-interest and to contrast the market with other milieus such as the family, the church, and the community, where behavior is more likely to be altruistic or at least sensitive to the needs of others. However, this common-sense distinction is misleading because each market transaction actually involves some mixture of self-interested action and other-regarding action.

People are willing to enter into market transactions because they have some basic level of trust that the other party is not going to cheat. There is a necessary element of reciprocity where both sides say that they are pursuing their self-interest but in a way that respects the other person. Obviously, con artists and criminal enterprises routinely betray this trust, but legitimate businesses are supposed to pursue their self-interest in a way that does not trample on the rights of others. Remember, for example, the universal outrage when United Airlines had a customer physically dragged out of his seat.

This trust does not just emerge spontaneously; the legal system actively works to assure that market participants operate with an acceptable level of respect for their counterparties. The legal rules that structure the behavior of market participants both enable and entitle them to act in a self-interested manner, but they also limit and constrain conduct so as to protect the interests of other market participants. The law of contracts, for example, involves an extended debate over what practices violate the requirement that the parties operate with "good faith." Where the lines are drawn will vary from one legal or historical context to another, and the precise location of the line can have significant distributional consequences.[1]

On a day-to-day basis, such lines are drawn by judges, but sometimes the legislature steps in, for example, to tighten laws against predatory mortgage lending in reaction to a judicial pattern of favorable treatment of mortgage companies at the expense of borrowers. Whether judicially or legislatively crafted, these changes in the ground rules of acceptable market behavior respond to political, cultural, and technological shifts. Some are minor in scope, but some, such as the reforms of the New Deal era, reflect major shifts in the balance of power.[2]

If actual markets require a combination of self-interested and other-regarding behaviors, it follows that there is no such thing as a singular logic to the market. Markets can produce very different outcomes depending upon the existing legal rules and the relative bargaining power of the parties. Take, for example, the market for rental housing. In Milwaukee, a city with about 105,000 renter households, about sixteen thousand people a year are evicted. Since this high rate of eviction is new, it is wrong to say that this is just the logic of housing markets, which requires that people get evicted when they don't pay rent.

Instead, as Matthew Desmond has recently shown, the very high rates of eviction are a relatively recent phenomenon that reflects stagnant wages at the bottom of the labor market, greater economic insecurity, the impact of the 1996 Personal Responsibility and Work Opportunity Reconciliation Act, and an ever-shrinking supply of public housing relative to ever-growing need.[3] An increasing number of families are spending 50 percent or more of their monthly income on rent. Milwaukee also differs from some other cities in that it has a legal regime that provides tenants with very few rights relative to landlords. Some cities protect renters through rules that limit the size of annual rent increases, and some have passed laws to contest arbitrary evictions and provide tenants with some additional time to pay an overdue rent bill.

Desmond provides a powerful example of a market that has generated a race to the bottom. The landlords he describes have incentives to keep raising prices and little incentive to respond to renter complaints about malfunctioning plumbing or broken windows. They know there are plenty of others desperate enough to rent a decrepit apartment. But some markets actually generate a race to the top as competition forces participants to provide more value to employees or consumers.

This happened with the labor market during World War II. Employers faced an acute shortage of skilled workers since the economy was running at full capacity for the war effort and millions had gone off to fight in Europe and Asia. With a wage and price freeze in effect, employers no longer had the option of raising wages to hold on to their employees, so they began using employee benefits as a tool to attract and retain employees. One important consequence was a big expansion in employer-provided health-care coverage, which continued into the postwar period.[4]

The point is that markets are complex institutions; a one-size-fits-all description is inadequate. Furthermore, it is problematic to speak of market values since markets depend on both the pursuit of self-interest and relations of trust with counterparties. To be sure, there are examples throughout history of people pursuing their self-interest with ruthlessness and utter disregard for the needs of others. But the most successful market economies have been those in which that kind of ruthlessness is contained and punished. In fact, countries where the wealthy are able to act with impunity have only rarely been able to produce the kind of dynamic economy that raises the standard of living for most people.

THE PROBLEM OF THE AUTONOMOUS ECONOMY

Since individual markets do not share a basic logic, it is wrong to think of them as being integrated into a single, unified, and autonomous market system. Nevertheless, this problematic idea has become a critical part of the baggage that comes with the concept of capitalism. Most economists conceptualize the profit-driven economic system as an autonomous mechanism that integrates the markets for labor, money, and products, and that is able to stand on its own and function independently of other social arrangements. This image has become part of the society's conventional wisdom; it is reflected in the widespread hostility to government "intervention" in the economy.

This perception or fantasy has very deep and dangerous consequences. Most people understand that the economy is not something concrete and visible, like Mount Everest or the Grand Canyon; it is an abstraction that encompasses some fraction of human activity. Our common sense is that when we are in bed in the morning and the alarm goes off, we are in the private sphere of family life. But by the time we get to work in the morning, even if it is a home office, we have entered the sphere of the economy, where we imagine that our actions and choices are shaped by the rationality of the market. However, the divide between the economy and the rest of social life is never a clean one.

At the beginning of the nineteenth century, the classical economists took the step of arguing that this abstract, analytical entity—the economy—is and should be largely independent of other aspects of social life. This was, of course, the justification for laissez-faire, or very limited government involvement in the economy. Since the economy is autonomous and governed by its own internal mechanisms, it must be allowed to self-regulate. Anything else will keep its internal laws from reaching the desired state of balance.[5]

Economists readily acknowledge that the concept of the autonomous economy is an abstraction. But they insist that proceeding "as if" the economy were something autonomous remains a very fruitful theoretical starting point.[6] Just as physicists abstract away from real-world factors such as friction and weather when they calculate the speed of a falling object, so economists abstract away from such real-world factors as culture and politics when they posit economic autonomy. They reason that since factors "internal" to the economy are doing most of the causal work, it makes sense to focus on them.

This view of the economy as autonomous has now become common sense on the right, including especially the activists of the Tea Party movement. They embrace the separation of market and state as fervently as many on the left believe in the separation of church and state.[7] Since the economy is a separate and autonomous and self-regulating sphere, the government must leave it alone. Government actions that are explicitly designed to protect private firms, such as the big Wall Street bailout engineered in the last months of the Bush administration, are seen as anathema, and a majority of Republicans in the House of Representatives voted against the measure even though their party's president and treasury secretary pleaded that failure to approve the legislation might cause another great depression.[8] One doesn't abandon the principle of separation of market and state just because there might be some bad consequences.

Those in the center and on the left do not share the Tea Party view of "intervention." They typically favor certain types of government intervention in the economy, such as environmental laws and tighter financial regulations. But the very language of intervention in itself rests on the idea of an autonomous economy. The word "intervention" suggests that the government is outside of the autonomous economy, so that when it enacts regulations, it is intervening in a sphere that has been operating according to its own principles.

But saying something is autonomous is very much like saying it has structural integrity; it can stand and operate on its own. When, for example, engineers come to inspect a bridge across a river, their job is to evaluate whether the bridge is structurally sound. Imagine if they said: "It is close to having structural integrity; let's proceed as if it were sound." That would be engineering malpractice since the driver of a sixteen-wheel tractor-trailer needs the bridge to be structurally sound in fact.

Actual developments in the financial markets leading up to the 2008 crash resembled such malpractice. As former Federal Reserve chair Alan Greenspan said in his famous mea culpa, "I might have put too much faith in the capacity of actors in the financial markets to regulate themselves."[9] He operated on the assumption that these markets were part of an autonomous economy that had structural integrity and could stand on its own. Imagine his surprise when the whole thing collapsed, like one of those highway bridges that periodically fails because of inadequate maintenance.

Yet Greenspan was simply following the logic of earlier theorists. Friedrich Hayek, one of the most influential free market theorists of the twentieth century, thought of the market economy as a spontaneous order. It was spontaneous "because it arises out of the individual wills of the participants, without any of them needing to possess knowledge of the whole." In Hayek's words: "The aim of the market order ... is to cope with the inevitable ignorance of everybody of most of the particular facts which determine this order. By a process which men did not understand, their activities have produced an order much more extensive and comprehensive than anything they could have comprehended, but on the functioning of which we have become utterly dependent."[10]

But think how strange this conceptualization is. There are no comparable arguments that other social institutions are autonomous and can stand on their own. Nobody would be foolish enough to claim that the family is an autonomous, self-organizing entity. It obviously depends on the economy and has been constructed historically by religious traditions and is maintained by hundreds of specific legal arrangements. While some argue that governments have a high degree of autonomy because of their monopoly on legitimate violence, they are not generally seen as freestanding. After all, governments depend on their ability to draw revenues from economic activity. But if it is obvious foolishness to see other social institutions as freestanding and autonomous, why is this status accorded to the economy?

The answer is that it is a deeply rooted way of thinking that we have inherited from as far back as the seventeenth century. John Locke argued that private economic contracts were natural and existed before there was government. It follows that these private contracts evolved into an economy that was conceptualized as a natural, spontaneous system of order existing independent of government.

Economic sociologists, including myself, have tried to challenge this way of thinking by arguing that the economy is always embedded in society, politics, culture, and ideas in much the same way that coal or precious minerals are found embedded in other rocks and can only be extracted with a good deal of force.[11] The problem with this metaphor is that one can ultimately disembed the coal or gold and refine it down to its pure level. But you cannot disembed the economy from other institutions without destroying it. Since the economic actors themselves have been produced by a culture that instills certain ideas and beliefs, a disembedded economy would have no people in it.

Here is a different metaphor. Imagine that the economy is simi-lar to a huge pile of sand, like giant dunes at the beach. It is just the ever-shifting aggregation of all of the economic activities of indi-viduals. It is constantly changing shape with the winds, the tides, and in response to people and animals moving over it. The idea of building anything out of a big autonomous pile of sand is out of the question. Yes, the sand might take a shape that looks like some kind of spontaneous order, but this order will not last. However, by combining the sand with other materials—such as wood, water, soil, and lime—it can be transformed into durable structures. One can make long-lasting paths by packing the sand tightly between wooden boards; one can build berms by mixing the sand with soil. Baking the sand with lime and water can produce sand-lime blocks that can be a strong and effective building material. By analogy, economic activity by itself can't build anything durable, but when combined with other materials—culture, politics, law, and ideas— economic activity can be transformed from shifting sand dunes into structures that are stable and useful.

The best real-world test of these competing ways of thinking occurred in Russia after the collapse of the Soviet system in 1991. Theorists of "shock therapy" were worried that the state's power-ful role in managing the Russian economy would reassert itself in the absence of rapid initiatives to move toward a market econ-omy.[12] They were not concerned that the people in Russia had little familiarity with how competitive markets work. They sim-ply assumed that if one moved quickly to privatize state-owned firms, a new market order would quickly and spontaneously emerge. They saw the market order as natural: when people were freed of the coercion of the old regime, they would quickly start doing what was natural—behaving like rational economic actors in a functioning market economy.

As the transformation began, a lot of people followed the injunction to make as much money as they could. In this sense, the shock therapists were successful in getting the new message across. But the ways in which people maximized their incomes were often not what the theorists had in mind. The elite of the old Soviet system—the nomenklatura—rushed to grab up ownership of state-owned businesses, but very few of them settled down to run those firms as ideal typical capitalists. Some literally packed up the machine tools and other equipment in their newly owned factories, put them in trucks that crossed Russia's international border, and sold them to the highest foreign bidders. Some gained control over valuable resources such as energy and raw materials; they did nothing to improve production but simply raised prices as much as possible. Still others hired criminal gangs to wage war on their competitors. In fact, instead of spontaneous order, there was an explosion of criminal activity. Kidnapping became a big business; the quickest way to make money was to grab other people and hold them for ransom. This, in turn, generated huge business opportunities for private security firms. Experienced military officers sold their services as security contractors, and it quickly became impossible to do business without hiring one or another of these firms to provide protection.[13]

The immediate consequence of shock therapy was that the bottom fell out of the economy. The old system was dismantled, but the new market economy was basically crippled by the violence and disorder of the transition period. Unemployment levels went through the roof, those who were employed were often not paid, and barter became common because people no longer trusted the existing currency and credit was completely unavailable. The country's GDP fell continuously from 1991 to 1998, even after the shock therapy approach was abandoned. After 1998, the Russian economy began to grow again, fueled primarily by sales of its abundant natural resources.

The prolonged 1990s crisis is a textbook case showing how the autonomous economy is little more than a sand dune. Shock therapists failed to understand that the successful market economies in Europe and North America were the product of the development over hundreds of years of political, legal, cultural, and ideational structures that support the functioning of productive markets.[14] These did not exist in Russia, so shock therapy produced not spontaneous order but rampant disorder. Most obviously, absent were the legal rules and enforcement systems that channel the pursuit of self-interest into business activity that increases the flow of goods and services. In this vacuum, people will make money the old-fashioned way—through extortion and predation.

THE FICTITIOUS COMMODITIES

Another way to understand how a market economy is dependent rather than autonomous is through the Central European social theorist Karl Polanyi's concept of fictitious commodities.[15] Polanyi argued that both the market economy and economic theory rest on the fiction that land, labor, and money are commodities that can be bought and sold in the market like anything else. Real commodities, he insisted, are those things that were initially produced for sale on the market such as a loaf of bread, a single-family home, a shiny new car. This is not true for land, labor, and money.

Land, he noted, is subdivided nature. With the minor exception of some low-lying areas reclaimed from the sea, people have to make do with the land that geological processes created. Even when demand is extremely high, nature does not respond by creating more of it. Similarly, labor is the activity of actual human beings who were not produced in response to market signals. To be sure, there have been times in history when people have responded to economic improvement by having larger families, but the opposite also happens, especially when people no longer rely on their children to support them in old age. Finally, in all modern economies, the supply of money and credit is managed by central banks that try to thread the needle between tight money, which cuts off economic activity, and excessive monetary expansion, which fuels inflation and asset price bubbles.

To be sure, we have elaborate systems in place to buy and sell land, labor, and money at prices that are determined by the market. Polanyi's point is that with real commodities, the price mechanism, by itself, can usually balance supply and demand, as, for example, when higher prices encourage producers to increase output at the same time that consumers also shift to cheaper substitutes. But since this mechanism does not occur with fictitious commodities, government necessarily plays an active role in coordinating the market for these key inputs into production.

With land, the market is structured by governmental rules over what types of activity are permitted in certain areas and by government provision of key infrastructure such as roads, bridges, tunnels, sewers, and water supply. Since it is almost always more profitable to develop land for housing rather than to use it for agriculture, most governments have acted to keep the market mechanism from bringing about too rapid a conversion of farmland into urban and suburban developments. Similarly, within cities, different areas are zoned for different activities, so that heavy industry does not pop up in the middle of prime residential neighborhoods. While those businesspeople who develop real estate at the local level might occasionally demand that government get out of their way, the reality is that government and business have to work hand in hand to support the market for land and new buildings.

In a parallel fashion, government plays a critical role in balancing supply and demand in the labor market. Public schools and colleges educate the labor force in an effort to avoid shortages of skills that are needed by employers. Publicly supported retirement programs help redistribute job opportunities from older workers to younger workers. Similarly, unemployment insurance and other forms of government assistance have been consistently used to adjust the supply and demand for labor. And, of course, governments also have long used immigration and emigration policies for the same purpose.

With money, a purely private banking system cannot assure the kind of steady growth of the supply of money and credit that avoids the twin dangers of runaway booms and crippling deflations. This is why all market economies have developed central banks that attempt to regulate this supply on a daily basis, and that includes limiting the credit creation of private financial institutions.[16]

Land, labor, and money do not even exhaust the category of fictitious commodities. Knowledge—or at least the kind of knowledge that can be used by business—is yet another fictitious commodity. Patents, copyrights, or licenses to use particular types of commodified knowledge are routinely traded on markets, but they differ fundamentally from ordinary commodities. For one thing, some of this valuable knowledge is produced as a byproduct when scientists attempt to solve puzzles that often have nothing to do with commercial applications. For another, the protection of intellectual property creates a system of government-imposed monopolies that eliminate standard competition and market-clearing prices.[17]

Polanyi's idea of fictitious commodities helps us to see that the creation of a market economy is a project of social engineering. The economy is not a natural entity obeying its own inner laws, but rather something that is constructed and reconstructed. The day-to-day government activity of managing fictitious commodities can be thought of as routine maintenance activity, but every now and then, new policies and new institutions are required to bring the supply and demand for fictitious commodities into balance; this would be the equivalent of remodeling projects. And, of course, these remodels can be more or less radical. When, for example, the U.S. created the Federal Reserve or when a new system for financing home mortgages was created in the 1930s, large parts of the old structure had to be gutted and redone.

This process of construction and reconstruction is ongoing and permanent; there is never some equilibrium where the economy is proceeding on its own. For example, over the last thirty years, market economies have had to adjust to the digitization of property—the existence of software programs, newspapers, books, games, movies, music, and art that consist of a complex sequence of digital codes. This shift has created a whole complicated set of legal questions because the old rules of property are simply inadequate to settle disputes created by the unique aspects of digital property, such as the fact that a particular program can be used by billions of people at the same moment.

Courts, legislators, and international bodies have been working overtime to establish new rules to govern this new type of property. We have seen the issue debated in the music industry with legal cases over websites that allowed peer-to-peer sharing of recorded music and in publishing with legal fights about digitizing whole libraries. While some visionaries argue that the capacity to share digital property should facilitate new forms of shared or collective ownership, others, including representatives of industry, have fought for tighter protection of their property rights. The point here is not to rehash these debates, but to recognize that societies face huge choices in constructing these new legal rules.[18]

CONTRADICTIONS OF GLOBALIZATION

The third part of the argument focuses on the way we conceptualize the global economy, which is often thought of as a global capitalist system. The same tendency to naturalize economic processes that occurs with individual markets and with national economies operates even more powerfully at the level of the global economy. Whether global capitalism is envisioned as an octopus with its tentacles reaching everywhere or as the goose that lays golden eggs, it is inevitably seen as a living, breathing organism. Nations that defy the organism's laws are bound to experience sharp declines in their standard of living or even total chaos. Moreover, these laws are assumed to leave almost no room for choice; they are seen as expressing the dynamic essence of a global capitalist system. It is part of the organism's logic to require free trade, free movement of capital, and a strictly limited role for government in managing the economy.[19]

All of this is mistaken. The global economy does have rules, but there is nothing natural or unchanging about them, and some of them are routinely and flagrantly ignored. Moreover, for several hundred years, the major shaper and enforcer of those rules has been a hegemonic global power—first England and then the United States. These powers do not have an owners' manual for global capitalism; those who make policy choices for the hegemonic powers simply stumble along trying as best they can to benefit their nation's businesses and their nation's citizens. And they frequently fail both in generating order and in benefiting their own citizens.

The history of these global rules has hardly been smooth or continuous; there have been periods of sharp discontinuity as an older order collapses or a new set of rules and institutions is put in place. Multiple factors shape this history. Throughout recorded history, there is a familiar pattern of great powers rising to international hegemony and then beginning a slow but relentless process of decline. Both England and the United States have conformed to this pattern. As their hegemonic advantage declines, they have both been confronted with challenges from rising powers with competing visions of international order. Moreover, a weakened hegemon has greater difficulty providing the global public goods that it had earlier promised. The consequence tends to be greater international economic disorder, and that tends to fuel demands for changes in the global order.

Global rules and global governance institutions are also subject to pressure from social movements. This pattern goes back to at least the eighteenth century, when the abolitionist movement in England began campaigning for an end to the global slave trade. The successful eighteenth-century struggles for national independence in the American colonies and in Haiti began a two-hundred-year campaign to reshape the world economy to eliminate colonialism and assure national self-determination. In our own time, a variety of global movements have had success in reshaping the global economic rules to combat environmental degradation and to expand the rights of women, workers, and indigenous peoples. Social movements have also forced changes in the global trade regime to increase the availability of medications to fight HIV/AIDS in the developing world.

In a word, the rules and institutions that govern the global economy are being constantly constructed and reconstructed as a consequence of shifts in global power balances, pressures from social movements, and the emergence of new technologies and new capacities. They have changed frequently in the past and there is every reason to believe that they can and will change in the future.

TRANSFORMATIONS IN THE ECONOMY'S CENTRAL ACTIVITY

As in the example of digitization of property, changes in production help to drive the process by which the economy is continuously being constructed and reconstructed. This is particularly obvious with advances in transportation; nobody doubts that the coming of the railroad, the automobile, and the airplane have had profound impacts on social organization. But the same is true of the arrival of the telegraph, the telephone, the internet, and the smart phone. Also important are the incremental advances in productivity in agriculture and manufacturing that have been going on for decades. Figure 1 shows that the yield in corn per acre has increased nearly sixfold since the 1930s, while figure 2 shows that real output per manufacturing worker in the U.S. rose almost eightfold in the sixty years from 1950 to 2010. Since the growth in population and in the demand for agricultural products and manufactured goods has risen far more slowly, this means that far fewer people are needed to work in farms and factories to produce the goods that we all consume. Figure 3 shows the decline in the

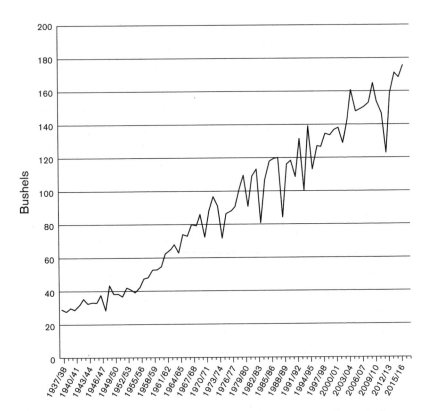

Figure 1. Corn yield per acre in the United States, 1937–2016. Source: United States Department of Agriculture, Economic Research Service, "Feed Grains: Yearbook Tables," uploaded December 13, 2016.

share of manufacturing employees as a percent of the economically active population.

Analysts of all political stripes argue that many of those U.S. manufacturing jobs simply moved to China and Mexico and other lower-wage locations. There is some truth to this, as anyone who has tried to buy a U.S.-made toaster or telephone or other small appliance knows. However, the contraction of the manufacturing

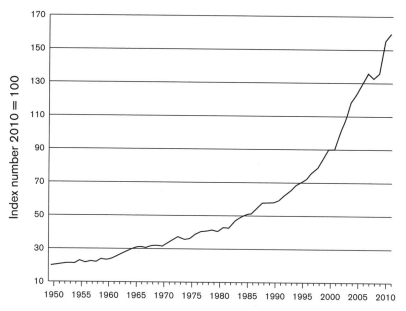

Figure 2. Output per employed person in manufacturing in the United States, 1950–2010. Source: U.S. Bureau of Labor Statistics, Output per Employed Person in Manufacturing in the United States, retrieved from FRED (Federal Reserve Bank of St. Louis). https://fred.stlouisfed.org/series/USAOPEP, January 4, 2017.

labor force is a global phenomenon that is impacting China, Mexico, Vietnam, and every other nation.[20] For example, automobile plants around the world now use just a hundredth of the labor time to produce each car as was used in such plants a century ago. In the 1930s, Ford's River Rouge plant had more than one hundred thousand employees. Today, the largest automobile plants rarely employ more than forty-five hundred workers. Factories in China are now rapidly introducing labor-saving technologies such as robotics, so average Chinese factory sizes are also falling.[21]

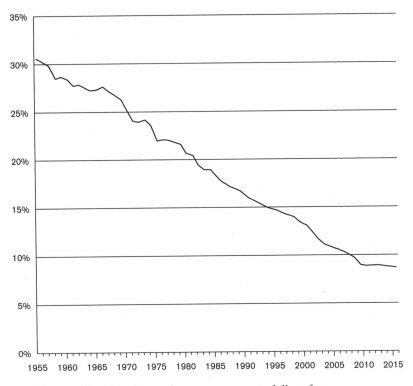

Figure 3. Manufacturing employment as a percent of all nonfarm employment, 1955–2015. Source: Bureau of Labor Statistics, Table B-1. Employees on nonfarm payrolls by industry sector and selected industry detail.

The contraction of employment in agriculture and manufacturing means that about 80 percent of people in the U.S. now work in the service sector—an umbrella category that includes public-sector work, nonprofits, education, health care, financial services, business services, retail trade, restaurants, tourism, and entertainment. This category encompasses the highest-paid people on Wall Street (e.g., hedge fund managers), the lowest-paid employees (e.g., workers in fast food or Walmart), and everybody in between. Because the category is heterogeneous, there is no inkling of a shared identity among people who do this kind of work. The service sector is basically just a residual category that means that one's labor does not produce a tangible and visible output such as a bushel of wheat or a ton of steel.

This residual nature of the service category has presented a big problem in trying to conceptualize what kind of society emerges when the manufacturing sector starts to shrink. For almost fifty years now, analysts have been using the term "postindustrial" to label the epoch that follows industrialism.[22] But the term has rarely been taken up by journalists, politicians, or business leaders, in part because it is abstract and lacks specificity. Agricultural society immediately makes one think of a farm, while industrial society evokes the factory. "Postindustrial" is really just a placeholder that points to something other than the farm or the factory.

Now, after almost fifty years, it is easier to see what has become the central economic activity of our society; it is creating, maintaining, and improving human habitation, or the social and physical environments in which most people live. Habitation is literally the act of living in a place, and for most of history, people attended to their habitation by creating villages, towns, and cities where they lived and worked. But creating habitation was always subordinated to such essential activities as farming, commerce, and manufacturing. Moreover, for centuries there has been a fundamental tension between habitation and economic progress.[23]

In England, for example, when landowners began pursuing more productive agricultural techniques in the centuries leading up to the Industrial Revolution, they enclosed the agricultural commons where smallholders had historically grazed their sheep.

The consequence was a severe disruption in the habitation of many rural people. These communities were disrupted once again as industrialization forced many to move to factories in crowded and polluted cities. And then when working people had finally re-created livable urban and small-town neighborhoods, their habitation was undermined yet again as factory jobs departed for cheaper labor in other places. But now, as producing and sustaining habitation becomes the central economic activity, it becomes possible to overcome this historic conflict between habitation and economic progress.

In the U.S. in 2014, less than 10 percent of a labor force of 150 million worked in agriculture or manufacturing. The key components of the habitation labor force are the 12 percent who work in health care and social assistance, the 15 percent who work in education or for state and local governments (including public school teachers), the 4.1 percent who work in construction, the 10.2 percent employed in retail trade, and many of the 12.7 percent who work in professional and business services. To be sure, the categories used in the available labor force data are not fine grained enough to clearly differentiate people whose work involves building and sustaining habitation. Arguably, the category should also include the 9.8 percent who work in leisure and hospitality, the 3.1 percent who work in transportation and warehousing, and the 1.8 percent in information.[24] But however one does the categorization, it seems clear that habitation is now the work of a majority of the labor force.

Since these people are simultaneously producers and consumers of habitation, they tend to benefit from technological advances that in earlier historical moments disrupted habitation. If society can learn to more efficiently improve communities, with better infrastructure and better services, people would experience simultaneously an improved standard of living, more leisure time, and better jobs. The logic that requires some people to live with a second- or third-rate habitation so that the rest of us can live more comfortably no longer holds.

In fact, a critical feature of this habitation society is the growing number of people in both the public and the private sectors whose work centers on innovation—developing new products and new processes for producing both goods and services. There was, of course, innovation in industrial society as big corporate laboratories hired scientists and technicians to develop new products. But there has been a qualitative change both in the scale of innovation activity and in its location. Nowadays, the innovation labor force is much larger and it is spread out across the public sector, big firms, small firms, universities, and government laboratories.[25] Moreover, the focus of innovation goes well beyond hardware, with an increasing emphasis on developing applications that fit with the project of improving habitation. For example, more sophisticated information management systems, including electronic medical records, are seen as central to the process of improving the effectiveness of health-care delivery, and many cities are experimenting with smart phone–based systems to coordinate both public and private transportation services. In short, as more and more people focus on habitation, there is a tendency for innovation to become ubiquitous.

A second qualitative change in a habitation society is the increasing centrality of infrastructure spending. In industrial society, infrastructure spending was important, but it was primarily an auxiliary to the mass production of agricultural and industrial goods. Substantial investments were needed for canals, railroads, harbors, navigable rivers, and highways in order to facilitate getting goods to markets. In the twentieth century, as suburbs grew, the major issue was facilitating the movement of employees to factories and offices.

In a habitation society, however, infrastructure spending ceases to be an auxiliary form of investment. On the contrary, investments in transportation systems, communication systems, energy systems, and water and water treatment systems are now critical. Moreover, the most dynamic cities are the ones that have invested in building and rehabilitating urban amenities, including parks, arts districts, museums, and other features that attract both locals and tourists. In fact, smart infrastructure spending is increasingly the key factor that differentiates successful regions from unsuccessful ones.[26] This is logical because good infrastructure can reduce various forms of waste, such as excessive outlays for fossil fuels and time lost in traffic jams, while also enhancing the quality of people's habitation.

BARRIERS TO AN EFFECTIVE TRANSITION

The problem is that we are moving into a habitation society with the mind-set and the institutions of the industrial era, and these keep us from realizing the benefits of this new type of economy. A habitation society creates the possibility of much greater equality, since prosperity no longer depends on large portions of the population doing mind-numbing work, but what we have instead is growing income and wealth inequality and large portions of the population experiencing ever greater economic insecurity. Our urban areas are increasingly divided between extremely expensive upscale neighborhoods that enjoy all kinds of amenities and marginalized neighborhoods with poor-quality schools, health care, and transportation. More and more people end up in distant suburbs, where they endure daily commutes of three or four hours to get to work. At the same time, rural areas and small towns continue to lose jobs and population as agricultural and industrial employment shrinks. These areas also often lack the communications infrastructure needed to attract new businesses, such as fast internet and cell phone towers.

A good way to see these contradictions is by examining infrastructure decisions specifically. In the industrial era, there were deliberate efforts to create technocratic structures that insulated infrastructure choices and spending from ordinary politics. The classic instances were the Port Authority of New York and New Jersey and the Triborough Bridge Authority—the foundation of the legendary power of Robert Moses. These technocratic arrangements were designed to reduce the corruption of big-city political machines and to facilitate better decisions about where roads and bridges and airports should be built.

But when habitation is what people are both producing and consuming, it is irrational to place infrastructure decision making outside of politics. There need to be new democratic mechanisms through which citizens are able to choose what kind of infrastructure they want their communities to have. One initiative along these lines is participatory budgeting, which began in Brazil but has now spread to countries around the world.[27] Citizens in different neighborhoods are provided the opportunity to influence how a city's infrastructure budget is allocated. But one can also imagine an even broader process through which citizens would be able to develop rival regional infrastructure plans and ultimately choose how their region develops.

However, our mechanisms for financing and justifying infrastructure outlays are hopelessly archaic. The problem is particularly acute because the cost of infrastructure is continually rising relative to total economic output, for two reasons. First, with transportation, communication, and energy, new technologies usually do not replace older ones; they are simply layered on top. So in transportation, for example, we have to maintain existing infrastructure and add new facilities for waterborne travel, railroads, highways, air travel, and now space travel.

Second, most types of infrastructure spending cannot realize the productivity gains that typically occur with mass production. Bridges and tunnels, for example, have to be tailored for a specific location, and even if some of the parts can be mass produced, much of the work of assembling those parts is labor intensive. There have been substantial productivity advances in construction activities, but they are far slower than the doubling of manufacturing output per worker between 1997 and 2010 (figure 2). The consequence is that infrastructure building and maintenance requires more labor than manufacturing, so the relative cost of most infrastructure projects tends to be high.

The combination of ever-expanding infrastructure needs with higher costs per project creates an infrastructure financing crisis. In the United States, where resistance to higher taxes has been particularly intense, the consequence is an infrastructure spending gap that is estimated at $2.0 trillion for the years 2016 through 2025.[28] With such a gap, it is extremely difficult to find funds for new infrastructure, while some of the existing infrastructure falls into a danger zone of disrepair. Among the consequences are bridge collapses, destroyed homes from flood damage, catastrophic fires caused by exploding rail cars, and lead in the drinking water supply of some cities. Moreover, the costs of dealing with the consequences of deferred maintenance on critical infrastructure are often many times greater than the cost of timely remediation.

But the bigger point is that in a habitation society, infrastructure investments are a critical driver of economic dynamism. Not surprisingly, the failure to make those investments results in a weaker economy and fewer employment opportunities. The result is a vicious downward spiral as tax revenues fail to rise while demands for government services continue to rise. Infrastructure spending would be the way out, but it becomes decreasingly feasible as the government faces an ever more intense fiscal crisis.

THE POLITICS OF HABITATION

The habitation labor force is still a heterogeneous category that encompasses people with widely different levels of compensation and social status and little in the way of shared identity. Nevertheless, there are definite indications of an emergent politics created by the growing centrality of habitation. The leading edge of this emergent politics has been the modern environmental movement, which differs from the earlier focus of conservationists on defending pristine wilderness and natural areas to emphasize instead the importance of cleaning the air, cleaning the water, and constructing more livable, sustainable, and resilient communities. In recent decades, the emergence of environmental justice movements indicates that these are not just middle-class issues; the desire for healthy and sustainable communities cuts across class and racial lines.

But the deeper reality is that a politics of habitation has the potential to bring some unity and coherence to different groups that have been waging seemingly unconnected struggles. In addition to various campaigns for environmental protection and environmental justice, there is the politics of care, the politics of place, and struggles for economic justice. The politics of care encompasses efforts to improve access and quality of services such as child care, education, health care, reproductive services, and parallel initiatives for paid family leave and other measures that would make it easier to balance work and family life. The politics of place includes mobilizations by communities for improved services and job opportunities as well as campaigns against racialized policing and crackdowns on the undocumented. Struggles for economic justice include fights for higher minimum wages and for a tax system that is not tilted in favor of the wealthy and giant corporations. The point is that all of these can be understood as complementary efforts to create a more inclusive, a more democratic, and a more egalitarian habitation society.

Moreover, the politics of habitation provides a framework for responding to the deepening political polarization between urban areas and less densely populated communities in rural areas and small towns. In virtually every part of the country, big cities and their suburbs, despite their considerable class and ethnic diversity, are increasingly Democratic in their voting patterns while support for the Republicans increases dramatically as one moves to counties with lower population density. This intense polarization plays out in state politics with Republican legislatures, elected through gerrymandering that increases the clout of their base voters, enacting measures that block more progressive initiatives passed by city governments.

There are, of course, many dimensions to this polarization, including racial animosity and cultural resentment against coastal elites, but a critical element is the stark reality that rural areas and small towns have largely been excluded from the economic growth of the last several decades. But this is precisely where this division maps onto politics in a completely paradoxical way. Less densely populated areas, whether entire states or counties within states, are generally tax takers, receiving substantially more than they pay at both the federal and the state level. Urban areas, in contrast, pay more in taxes than they get back from government programs.

It would make sense for people in less densely populated areas to exploit this situation by forcing higher taxes on urban voters to finance more of the infrastructure and services they need. But they have done exactly the opposite. They have thrown their votes to a political party that has pushed for lower taxes across the board, creating a generalized fiscal crisis that restricts spending on both sides of this divide. There are policy choices that would improve habitation in both more and less dense communities, but those choices are not on the agenda because of the failure to recognize the need for a deeper reform of political and economic institutions that includes changing both the level and the structure of taxation.

This is only one example of a dynamic of misrecognition that occurs as people seek to respond to economic problems through the obsolete categories and concepts of an earlier epoch. Another example centers on our way of thinking about the economy's output. The system of national economic accounting that most nations use to monitor their economy's health is a modestly revised version of the accounting scheme that was developed in the 1930s and 1940s, when the majority of employees worked on farms or in factories. Economic output was defined as the dollar value of tangible outputs purchased by consumers. The metric simply ignored the self-provisioning work that consumers did in the home, as well as the positive and negative impacts of economic activity on the environment, and it assumed that the output of public-sector workers and many in the service sector could be approximated by their wages.

In a habitation society, this system of economic measures produces increasingly unreliable results.[29] For example, the United

States spends about $3 trillion per year on health care, but the improvement in health-care outcomes is not counted as part of economic output. And yet we know that life expectancy after sixty has risen significantly over recent decades, and there have been significant gains in the health status of many people in their fifties, sixties, and seventies. (Improvements in health status mean lower rates of disability and greater ability to perform a wide range of tasks.) To be sure, the U.S. health-care system wastes vast amounts of money, and there are also some important counter-trends, such as rising rates of obesity, diabetes, and heightened mortality rates for middle-age white men with a high school education. Nonetheless, it is problematic to measure economic output in a way that ignores changes in the health of the population.[30]

These various forms of misrecognition are connected. So, for example, even though infrastructure spending has become increasingly central in a habitation society, its economic contribution is understated in the official economic indicators. When a decaying bridge is replaced by a much-improved structure, the gain in safety or even the reduction in traffic congestion is not reflected in the economic data. So why should political leaders make a big investment in an infrastructure upgrade that won't move the key indicators that are used to evaluate economic performance?

But in a habitation society, the key variables are increasingly qualitative and difficult to measure. The desirability of a particular urban neighborhood, for example, is not captured by variables such as amount of park space per resident. Everything hinges on the quality of the parks or the specific mix of amenities that can easily be accessed. The story of education is similar. Nobody really cares anymore how many years of schooling somebody has had; the important question is the quality of the schooling, the particular mix of skills and knowledge that the individual has gained. This shift means that the use of the crude measurement instruments of the industrial era is bound to be misleading.

CONCLUSION

What I have tried to suggest in this chapter is an institutional and historical way of thinking about the economy that is very different from the social theory that is now part of the baggage associated with the word "capitalism." In place of the usual tendency to understand markets and the market system as natural entities, I have stressed that they are constructed and are constantly in need of reconstruction. Similarly, most discussions of capitalism assume that the system operates pretty much the same regardless of what is being produced. I argue instead that the shift in the central economic activity from producing food to producing manufactured goods to producing human habitation has huge implications for the way society should be organized.

CHAPTER THREE

The Illusion That Democracy Threatens the Economy

The single most dangerous illusion that comes with the prevailing concept of capitalism is the idea that too much democracy is a threat to economic prosperity. Many in our political and economic elites believe that democracy must be restrained and limited if we are going to have a well-functioning capitalist economy. This view is disastrously wrong; market economies have flourished precisely because of the positive interaction between markets and political democracy. Successful efforts to restrain democracy yield highly negative economic consequences.

Current skepticism about democracy echoes views that prevailed at the founding of the Republic. The Federalist Papers express the idea that democratic institutions constitute a deep and continuing threat to the existence of a productive and efficient economy. The problem, stated baldly by James Madison, is that the mob of those without property will impose excessive taxation on the productive class, destroying their incentive to engage in entrepreneurial activity.[1] The proposed solution is to recognize and reinforce the autonomy of the economy, so that it is effectively walled off from democratic influences. In a word, the needs of a market economy, not the preference of voters, should shape government action. Democracy should largely be irrelevant when it comes to setting economic policies because basic economic laws such as supply and demand cannot be over-ruled by electoral majorities.

Many of the Founders wanted to emulate England and restrict the franchise to men who owned property and would stand against the mob. While such restrictions proved untenable, they designed the Constitution to protect the political process from the influence of those without property. The separation of pow-ers among the executive, legislative, and judicial branches was seen as a critical bulwark against the poor. Even if populist forces gained control of one or two branches, their momentum could be halted by the remaining branch. Moreover, the United States Senate was modeled on the English House of Lords to assure that property holders could slow down or block legislation that was thought to be too threatening to the autonomy of the economy. This was accomplished by six-year terms for senators and the provision that mandated the selection of each state's senators by their own state legislature. Direct election by voters of senators did not arrive until the passage of the Seventeenth Amendment to the Constitution in 1913.

These fears of the Founders have persisted over many dec-ades.[2] When the Federal Reserve was established as the nation's central bank in 1913, elaborate steps were taken to insulate the Fed from congressional oversight and influence so that mone-tary policy would not reflect the pressure for inflation from those with little property and lots of debt. Conservative oppo-nents of Franklin Roosevelt's New Deal insisted that legislation such as the Social Security Act and the National Labor Relations

Act would destroy the nation's economic vitality. Those claims were largely ignored, but when the U.S. economy suffered from stagflation in the 1970s, the idea that too much democracy damages the capitalist system came roaring back.

A widespread version of the argument insists that politicians gain office by promising voters benefits that their society cannot possibly afford. Pressure groups such as unions or organizations of the elderly make deals with politicians by trading their votes for expanded benefits. But the costs of these "entitlement" programs are alleged to be huge. Either taxes must be increased to pay the cost or the government must run a chronic deficit. Both higher taxes and government deficits, in this view, inevitably discourage enterprise and new investments and thus undermine the vitality of a capitalist economy.[3]

It follows logically that democratic societies must take steps to protect the economy from the electorate. One solution is to keep politicians from succumbing to these electoral pressures by imposing the requirement that government budgets be balanced each year, with no deficit spending allowed. Such balanced budget provisions are part of the constitution of many of the U.S. states and have been institutionalized in Germany, Italy, and Switzerland. The European Community has imposed on its members a strict limit on the total ratio of government debt to gross domestic product. In the U.S., advocacy of such a balanced budget rule at the federal level has been a conservative demand for years. These balanced budget provisions usually allow exceptions in case of war or other emergencies. But to prevent routine exceptions, they usually require a supermajority, often placed at two-thirds of both legislative houses, to pass an unbalanced budget or to raise tax levels.

The current structure of global economic governance reflects this same idea, that popular sovereignty must not be allowed to disrupt the core workings of market economies. When nations go to the International Monetary Fund for assistance, their governments are routinely told that they must reverse previous legislative enactments such as pension programs because they are inconsistent with a healthy economy. Similarly, in the recent Eurocrisis, the European Community forced parliaments in various nations to reverse previously enacted legislation. Signatories to the World Trade Organization agree in advance not to make use of certain policy options that might be popular with voters such as subsidies to support industries that create jobs. And the dispute resolution mechanism embodied in a number of international trade agreements gives foreign corporations the right to sue in special tribunals when legislatures pass regulatory measures that might be popular with voters but that negatively impact a particular corporation's investment in that country.[4]

This deep suspicion of democracy, shared by elites and much of the right, has produced powerful limitations on popular sovereignty at the subnational, national, and global level. This suspicion rests on the problematic idea that a capitalist economy is something autonomous that must be free to obey its own special laws if it is to produce prosperity. But this widespread conception of an autonomous economy is an illusion; the relationship between democracy and markets is far different.

A CONTRARY VIEW

The argument I am making is an unconventional one. Many on the center and the right argue that capitalism and democracy are highly compatible as long as the proper restraints are placed on popular sovereignty. Some leftists, as well, have argued that representative democracy is the perfect governing mechanism for a capitalist society precisely because parliaments and congresses prevent the people from exercising real power that would threaten the wealthy. My argument, in contrast, is that the more democratic a society becomes, the more effectively its market economy will work. There is no trade-off; each forward step in democratic governance helps to make the economy more productive and more dynamic.[5]

There are, in fact, very few examples of market economies flourishing over an extended period of time without the existence of democratic institutions. Germany, Japan, the Soviet Union, South Korea, and Taiwan made very rapid economic progress under monarchies or dictatorships, but in each of these cases, a limit was reached. With Germany and Japan, internal tensions led political leaders to gamble on military aggression that ended in humiliating defeats and the imposition of democracy from the outside. In the case of the Soviet Union, economic dynamism disappeared as the economy moved from extensive growth to intensive growth. In South Korea and Taiwan, economic growth fostered democratizing movements that allowed for continued economic success. Only those nations that opened themselves up to democratic participation were able to hold on to a dynamic and growing economy.

The great exception, of course, is China, which has experienced thirty-five years of rapid economic growth under the dictatorship of the Communist Party. China is exceptional because of its unique combination of a very strong central government and its extraordinarily large population size. This combination made it possible for China's leaders to negotiate particularly advantageous deals with foreign investors that were not possible for other nations. But even with these advantages, China is now struggling to maintain its high growth rate, which might mean that China is now facing the limits of economic success under authoritarian leadership.

How do we explain the affinity between strong market economies and democratic governance? One premise of my argument is that democratic institutions have consistently been won through popular pressure from below. Those with wealth have never been enthusiastic about allowing everyone to vote to elect legislatures that have the power to curb their privileges through taxes and regulation. In the U.S., the Founders generally wanted to restrict the vote to those with property, as was the practice in England. It was only the agitation by those without property, many of whom had been the foot soldiers of the Revolution, that resulted in the franchise being extended to all white men. The ongoing battle to extend the franchise to all citizens, regardless of wealth, gender, race, literacy, disability, or criminal convictions, has been waged from below, with propertied interests often resisting. Even today, billionaires in the U.S. finance concerted efforts to discourage minority and young voters by passing strict voter identification laws in the states.

Moreover, there is a repeated historical pattern in which elements of the business elite respond to threats to their economic interests by throwing their support to political leaders who ignore democratic and constitutional restraints. This happened in the mid-nineteenth century in France with Louis Bonaparte, Napoleon III, and in the mid-twentieth century with fascist dictatorships. The U.S. has so far escaped the full descent into authoritarian rule, but with Richard Nixon and now again with Donald Trump, there has been significant business collusion with leaders who threaten to undermine democratic institutions. This means, in turn, that both the creation and the preservation of democratic institutions depends on pressures exerted by ordinary citizens who mobilize in defense of democratic institutions.

The second premise is that these democratic institutions counter the powerful drift of market societies toward oligarchy, or rule by the rich alone.[6] This is a very serious problem for the economy because oligarchic societies are not economically dynamic; they usually experience slow growth. This drift toward oligarchy exists because the market economy is not autonomous; it is constantly being shaped by government decisions that inevitably benefit some businesses and hurt others. The problem is that successful firms recognize this and they often invest some of their profits to influence public officials to favor them in those decisions.

At last count, there were 10,882 registered lobbyists in Washington, D.C., who were mostly representing business interests, and this figure significantly understates the number of full-time private-sector employees whose job it is to get government officials to make rulings that are favorable to their clients.[7] At the local level, politics tends to revolve around coalitions of real estate interests, developers, and construction firms that are hoping that when their people win office, the projects that they have been pushing for will be given a green light.

The history of Google provides an interesting case study in this process. Begun by graduate students at Stanford, Google adopted the slogan "Don't be evil," which was intended to differentiate their firm from corporate behemoths such as Microsoft, which were seen as ruthlessly pursuing their self-interest. In the early years, Google resisted engaging in any kind of political involvement, believing that if its technology remained superior, the firm would prosper. But as Google grew, it became impossible to sustain this disengagement from politics. Both in foreign countries and in this one, governments were every day making critical decisions that were influencing the company's future prospects. The firm reversed course and set up a Washington, D.C., operation and has become deeply involved in influencing politicians and government officials.

There is nothing surprising about business firms courting influence with politicians. We often think of this largely in terms of corruption; it is something ugly that we wish would go away. On the right, activists believe that if government would stay out of the private sector's business—if only there could be a rigid wall of separation between politics and government—then none of this would happen. But that is an impossible fantasy; government has no choice but to make decisions that create specific winners and losers in the business community. Others imagine that this problem would be solved by a system of public financing of political campaigns. Such a reform might eliminate some of the most serious abuses, but it would not stop the intertwining of business and politics.

While this intertwining of business and government is inevitable, it also creates the drift toward oligarchy. To work optimally, a market system requires firms to compete on a level playing field, so that victory goes to the firm that is most efficient in its use of resources. As with Darwinian evolution, market competition is supposed to reward the efficient, punish the inefficient, and create continuous pressure on all firms to improve. But a firm that is initially efficient can take some of its profits and invest them in gaining political influence. In exchange for campaign contributions or lucrative jobs for members of his or her family, the politician arranges for a subsidy that benefits that firm for the next twenty years. The firm no longer has to worry that much about efficiency because with the subsidy, it can remain profitable even if its efficiency sinks below the industry average. The same firm might then take another chunk of its profits and seek another deal with a politician in another jurisdiction. Through this strategy, the firm can continue to prosper without worrying about being more efficient than its competitors.

In short, the intertwining of politics and markets gives firms a choice; they can either continue to focus on being as efficient as possible or they can try to translate profits into political influence so that their market superiority becomes entrenched through favorable political rulings. The dirty secret is that nobody really likes to be banging away on a level playing field, week after week, month after month, year after year, trying to maximize the efficiency with which they use resources. In fact, much of contemporary business theory elaborates strategies by which firms try to tilt the playing field in their own favor. For example, creating brand loyalty allows established firms to avoid competing directly with lower-cost producers. But many of the favored strategies involve drawing on government support, such as gaining a monopoly over a given technology through the patent system, winning lucrative government contracts, gaining tax breaks, or taking advantage of loopholes in existing regulations.

The reality is that most businesses that can afford to wield political influence will try to do so. This accelerates the drift toward oligarchy. The richest firms and the richest individuals have the most resources to invest in political influence, and they try to tilt the playing field permanently in their own favor. They press for measures that entrench their firm's dominant position and make it impossible for challengers to compete with them. They also use political influence to get away with imposing costs on others, including paying substandard wages, damaging the environment, cheating customers, and permitting other forms of predatory behavior. The result is a much less efficient and attractive version of market society.

This is where political democracy enters the picture in a big way. Political democracy, instead of being a perpetual threat to the viability of market systems, is what protects market systems from drifting toward oligarchy. Democracy provides the opportunity for voters and outsider business interests to push back against government officials who want to subsidize established firms or permit them to impose unreasonable costs on others. Citizens can use democratic politics to level the playing field so that market competition does not become a rigged game.

There is a great irony here. For at least a generation, the most influential proposals for fixing our current economy favor cutting back on democracy to insulate the economy from the will of the citizenry. Influential voices have repeatedly denounced government entitlement programs such as Social Security and Medicare as resulting from illicit deals between self-interested politicians and greedy citizens. The Supreme Court has greatly enhanced the political clout of the wealthy by insisting that limits on campaign contributions violate the Constitution. But all of these measures designed to diminish popular sovereignty accelerate movement toward oligarchy and a less dynamic economy.

THE REAL DIVIDE: TWO TYPES OF MARKET SYSTEMS

One of the reasons that the term "capitalism" is so problematic is that it obscures the difference between two distinct types of market systems. Both of these systems fit the classic definitions of capitalism; each has private ownership of the means of production and each incentivizes business owners to maximize profits. But they are fundamentally different in their core economic dynamics. The first type, often referred to as "crony capitalism," I prefer to label as oligarchy. Oligarchy is rule by the twenty or fifty or hundred leading families and business groups. It can work either with an autocratic regime such as a monarchy or a dictatorship, or with a limited democracy where the people occasionally get to choose which faction of the elite will control the government. The second type is a genuine egalitarian democracy with a broad electorate that is able to exercise effective control over government at all levels.

Oligarchies will have slower rates of economic growth than egalitarian democracies for three key reasons. First, the dominant group of firms has little incentive to invest much in upgrading their production facilities because they face little direct competition. Their influence over government officials allows them to discourage competition through some combination of subsidies, tariffs, and regulatory measures that block new firms. At the same time, newer and smaller firms face such a hostile environment that their aggregate level of investment also remains low. This means low rates of innovation because the deck is effectively stacked against newcomers. Members of the existing elite might occasionally invest in something new, but this still means a much slower rate of change than occurs in more open systems.

Second, it is almost always easier for firms to make profits by shifting costs onto others than by increasing efficiency. Under oligarchy, the dominant firms and families often shift costs onto employees by paying low wages and maintaining dirty and dangerous work conditions, or they shift costs onto the environment through dumping their waste into water, air, or landfills. Third, the intertwining of government and the business elite characteristically produces a very unequal distribution of the nation's income. With the bottom 90 percent of the population receiving half or less of total income, ordinary people lack the purchasing power to fuel a vigorous consumer economy.

In contrast, market systems with egalitarian democracy tend to produce higher rates of economic growth for longer periods of time. While such societies also have large established businesses that lobby the government to defend and protect their interests, significant counterpressures limit the influence these firms exert. With greater transparency, lobbyists on behalf of labor unions, consumers, environmentalists, and small business are able to push back and challenge corporate rule. These challenges can force firms to focus on greater efficiency because regulations block the strategy of making profits by shifting costs onto others. At the same time, smaller and newer firms are able to get heard in the political process, and they are sometimes able to find support within government. This increases the possibility of innovation since the entrepreneur who "builds a better mousetrap" has a chance to attract consumers. And with the people having a greater voice in the political system, income distribution is more equal and consumers have greater purchasing power, and this produces greater economic dynamism.

If these ideal types sound somewhat familiar, it is because they are taken from one of the most famous books about the U.S. This is Alexis de Tocqueville's classic, *Democracy in America*.[8] While people of all political persuasions generally cite Tocqueville reverentially, his core argument tends to be either forgotten or ignored. The French aristocrat who traveled through the country in the 1830s was struck by the contrast between his native country and the U.S. Northern states. He saw France as an oligarchic system in which elite domination of politics and the economy led directly to stagnation. In the northern U.S., in contrast, the egalitarian ethos and democratic institutions generated a vibrant and dynamic economy; he saw the South as stagnant and oligarchic.

Tocqueville saw in the North a culture of enterprise in which people in all ranks of society believed in self-improvement and upward mobility. The absence of deference toward their superiors made people willing to try new things, and this created a broad culture of invention and entrepreneurship. In contrast to France, lots of ideas and initiatives bubbled up from below. All of this, of course, was supported by the frontier, which made free land available for those who were willing to face the risks of heading to the West. The frontier operated as a kind of universal safety net; people were willing to take more risks because if a new business failed, they had the option of starting out again on the frontier with a decent-sized piece of land. This also meant that lots of employees brought this same enterprising spirit to the workplace. Many saw their work for an employer as an apprenticeship during which they would learn a set of skills so that they could ultimately start their own business. But in the meantime, they wanted to do more than obey; they wanted to help their employer create a successful business.

Another feature of this enterprising culture was an emphasis on education and self-improvement. Public investments in higher education began very early with the federal government's creation of West Point and the development of state universities. The first public schools were created in Boston and the world's first system of public education expanded steadily thereafter. Mechanics' institutes and self-help organizations sprang up in many places to help working people gain higher levels of skill.

Tocqueville did not emphasize that this public culture of innovation was facilitated from the very beginning by the federal government. The U.S. patent office required that patent applications include a physical model of the proposed device, and these models were put on display in the patent office. This required the construction of a huge building to hold the models, begun in 1836 and not completed until 1867. This structure, referred to as a "temple of invention," suffered a fire that destroyed some eighty-seven thousand of the models in 1877. But this temple was not some antiquarian exercise to preserve the past; on the contrary, it was understood as a concrete way to support and facilitate the process of inventing new things. People would come to the museum, examine the models, and return home to develop their own inventions.[9]

But Tocqueville noted that this much broader class of entrepreneurs—unfazed by deference to their "superiors"—often sought help and support from politicians at the local, state, or federal levels. While government was supposed to just stay out of the way as entrepreneurs launched their initiatives, in practice, many of these businesspeople sought and received assistance from some level of government. Tocqueville emphasizes the plans for canals and railways to facilitate the expansion of commerce between the East Coast and the interior of the country. Since these projects often had considerable economic potential, both state legislators and Congress often provided assistance in the form of loans to support these efforts.

Tocqueville has a wonderful footnote that references the relationship between these kinds of entrepreneurial projects and government:

> At such times there are always a multitude of men engaged in difficult or novel undertakings, which they follow alone, without caring for their fellow-men. Such persons may be ready to admit, as a general principle, that the public authority ought not to interfere in private concerns; but by an exception to that rule, each of them

craves for its assistance in the particular concern on which he is engaged, and seeks to draw upon the influence of the government for his own benefit, though he would restrict it on all other occasions.[10]

The quote conveys a longstanding national trait, a deep belief that laissez-faire is a good principle that should apply to everyone else, but an exception should be made for one's own project, which is so obviously meritorious that it deserves governmental support. But in an egalitarian democracy, access to government officials is widely diffused and there are multiple levels of government to which one can appeal. Again, the contrast with France is dramatic. That country also had ambitious people who wanted to build canals and railroads, but the high degree of political centralization meant that the chances of getting state support were restricted to a far smaller group of upper-class citizens.

Moreover, economic growth over the last two centuries has involved a continuous series of major breakthroughs in transportation and communications technologies. Each of these critical technologies requires very substantial infrastructure investments that vastly exceed what individual firms could conceivably afford. In almost every country, government has been called upon to play a critical role in supporting this infrastructure either by funding it directly or by finding ways to coordinate and subsidize the efforts of private firms. Part of the reason for the long-term economic success of the United States is that its government has been aggressive in its efforts to support this kind of infrastructure development, often decades before other nations enter the competition. From Lincoln's commitment to building the intercontinental railroad through to the government's leadership role in creating the internet, this has been a key element in U.S. prosperity.

This is yet another part of the enterprising culture that Tocqueville identified in the 1830s. The combination of a broad stratum of entrepreneurs, the openness of government at multiple levels to the influence of businesspeople, and a bias in favor of the new have combined to maximize government's orientation toward constructing the infrastructure needed to support new technologies. Here again, democracy is not the enemy of economic dynamism; it has proven over and over again to be its most powerful ally.

THE FUNCTION OF HYBRIDITY

All of this illustrates that it has not been pure, unalloyed market systems that have flourished; rather, dynamism has been characteristic of hybrid market systems that are continually modified by pressures from democratic politics. When the market system is left to its own internal dynamics, it is subject to a process of degeneration that is generally ignored in economics textbooks. That wonderful state of competition among many different firms that are singly incapable of influencing the price structure tends to be of short duration. The more successful firms gradually get larger and larger, either through mergers and acquisitions or simply by driving their competitors out of the marketplace. As their size increases, they see the advantages of locking in profits by finding paths to profits that are protected from any kind of competition and by shifting costs onto others through sweating workers or contributing to environmental degradation. Since their size generates profits and political influence, they have both the incentive and the capacity to get political rulings that support these shortcuts to continuing profitability. Without strong democracy, this degenerative process saps the economy of its dynamism.[11]

But by wedding the market system to the radically different principles of political democracy, we get a hybrid that can limit this process of degeneration so that dynamism in the economy continues. The United States pioneered this productive hybrid by being the first major nation to create an electoral democracy that gave the right to vote even to indigent white men. To be sure, at the nation's founding, this democratic system was deeply compromised by slavery, racial and gender exclusion, and the various measures that the Founders had instituted to limit popular sovereignty. And yet, the combination of democratic principles, the separation of powers, and the political rights guaranteed in the Constitution created mechanisms for extending the franchise and dismantling at least some of those limits to popular sovereignty.

It is not just the formal mechanisms of democracy such as voting, political parties, and constitutional arrangements that are important, though. Informal mechanisms such as social movements also play a hugely important role in egalitarian democracy's economic benefits. This is critical because electoral competition, like market competition, can be vulnerable to a process of degeneration. This is a particularly serious danger in countries like the U.S., where electoral competition is effectively restricted to two major political parties. Dominant political parties can become very tightly linked to the concerns of particular interest groups and particular constituencies, and this leads them to ignore potential new constituencies. These ignored voters have the option to start a new political party, but the odds of electoral success for such a party are usually very limited. For this reason, social movements and protest activity are the major mechanism by which groups that lack influence within the two existing parties are able to get heard and are sometimes able to force the party system to respond.

Protest activity by social movements is made possible by the existence of democratic rights and a democratic culture. In the U.S., social movement activity has repeatedly played a major role in overcoming barriers to economic dynamism. Two classic instances are the abolitionist movement in the nineteenth century and the civil rights movement in the twentieth. As already indicated, virtually all the dynamism that Tocqueville identified in the U.S. was absent in the slave states; they were the U.S. version of oligarchy. An elite group of owners dominated both the economy and the polity, preserved an extremely inefficient form of agriculture, and blocked most forms of innovation. To be sure, the cotton economy was enormously profitable, but the plantation holders had little interest in reinvesting their profits in new technologies and new products. Moreover, any internal opposition to the Southern elite was easily marginalized or crushed. At the national level, all the government could do was manage a series of compromises that left slavery intact in the South and slowed its expansion into new territories.

The challenge to this system came in the form of abolitionism, which began as a fringe movement but ultimately led to the creation of the Republican Party and Lincoln's election to the presidency. The policies that Lincoln pursued, including the waging of the Civil War, the signing of the Emancipation Proclamation, the building of the intercontinental railroad, and the creation of the Department of Agriculture and the Land Grant universities, all played a critical part in the rapid economic growth that occurred in the decades after the Civil War. It was social movement activity of abolitionists that ended slavery and swept away the barriers to a dynamic, continental economy that emerged at the end of the nineteenth century as a global economic power.[12]

But as we know, the triumphant Northern states quickly tired of the task of forcibly modernizing Southern society. With this waning of political will, Reconstruction was brought to an end and the old Southern oligarchy was able to reclaim power by stripping African Americans of their newly granted rights. Jim Crow was put in place and many former slaves continued to raise cotton in conditions of servitude as sharecroppers. The consequence was that the states of the Old Confederacy experienced slower economic growth and more severe poverty than the rest of the nation.

The South remained largely entombed in an oligarchic time warp even as World War I and World War II drew many African Americans out of the comparatively stagnant region. The creation of the Tennessee Valley Authority and massive government spending during World War II began to accelerate economic growth, but it was once again social movement activity that weakened the power of the oligarchy and began the modernization of the region. The activism of the Southern civil rights movement in the 1950s and 1960s was critical in dismantling segregation, ending the exclusion of blacks from the electoral process, and destroying the one-party rule of Democrats. Gradually, parts of the South began to look like other parts of the country, with a better-educated and more highly integrated labor force, higher rates of business investment, and more dynamic economic growth.[13]

To be sure, even this "Second Reconstruction" was incomplete as the movement of Southern whites into the Republican Party in the 1970s and 1980s once again left Southern blacks in many localities with very limited political power. Many of the poorest counties in the nation continue to be located in the states of the Old South, and Alabama, Mississippi, and Arkansas remain at the bottom of most measures of income and well-being. Nevertheless, the region as a whole has experienced greater economic dynamism over the last fifty years than in earlier periods of its history, and much of this can be directly attributed to the civil rights movement.

GIVING PEOPLE WHAT THEY WANT

There is yet another reason that the hybrid combination of democracy and markets has proven to be so productive. Proponents of the market systems insist that the ability of consumers to choose what they want in the marketplace generates positive synergies. The obvious contrast is with the kind of central planning that existed in the old Soviet system, where government planners decided how much and what type of toothpaste to produce and consumers had very limited choice. That system produced shortages of some things, surpluses of others, poor-quality goods, and low levels of consumer satisfaction that fed back into a relatively unproductive labor force. Soviet employees would say: "They pretend to pay us and we pretend to work." In contrast, the market system allows employees to exercise choice in the consumer market place and this makes it possible—in many cases—to match precisely their consumption dollars with their personal needs. This matching, in turn, helps turn those consumers into more satisfied and more productive employees.

This argument about consumer sovereignty is often used for very conservative purposes. When advocates for public health or for environmental protection propose taxes on cigarettes or soda or carbon-based fuels, conservatives argue that such measures would interfere with the sovereign choices of consumers. But holding on to this core insight that it is economically beneficial when people are able to get the things they want and need forces us to reconsider much of the standard critique of the growth of state spending. The fundamental point is that some of the things that people want the most are not freely available to them on the market at a price they can afford. Key examples are a decent education for one's children, access to health care, and income security, which protects one from both predictable losses of income such as old age or infirmity as well as unemployment, health crises, or natural disasters.

In theory, people could purchase these things on the market, but this doesn't happen because the price is usually too high. Moreover, the whole business of providing insurance does not fit well into market theory. It is part of the logic of competitive markets that some firms will inevitably fail and go out of business. So what is to happen to the people who buy insurance policies from firms that later end up in bankruptcy? Nobody likes saying to the insured: "Tough luck, you trusted in the wrong firm. They went bankrupt so now you get nothing." In practice, this problem has been "solved" by government guarantees of the coverage that consumers purchase. But this only confirms the basic point that markets by themselves cannot provide these benefits. When private insurance is available, it is only because a government has decided to backstop the firms selling it.

Precisely because markets cannot provide universal access to education or health care or income security, people have used the machinery of democracy to fill these needs. Rather than viewing this as the creation of dangerous entitlements, we should see this as another illustration of the benefits of consumer sovereignty. Citizens use a combination of market purchases and strategic voting to get the mix of goods and services they want. Moreover, their ability to fill their needs—either through the market or through government—makes them, in turn, more productive, resulting in a more productive and dynamic economy.

To be sure, these forms of public provision vary greatly across different developed societies. The U.S. was a global innovator in creating a universal public school system extending from kindergarten to advanced degrees. However, it has been a global laggard in providing universal access to health care. Moreover, some of its key income security policies are dramatically less generous than those available in other developed democracies. But this variation is useful for our purposes because it allows us to evaluate the hypothesis that when people are able to satisfy their needs through public programs, it makes them and their society more productive.

Conservatives insist that "entitlement programs" that reduce the uncertainty and insecurity that individuals face in the marketplace make people passive and they lose the self-reliance that is needed to be productive in a market economy. They also assert that since such programs are extremely expensive to maintain, they require high rates of taxation. Conservatives insist that high taxes will discourage entrepreneurial activity and assure that a nation's products are less competitive in the global marketplace since the taxes have to be incorporated in the pricing of exported goods and services.

Such arguments have been quite explicit in discussions of "Eurosclerosis." The claim is that over the last few decades, European nations have had lower rates of new employment growth than the U.S. because of Europe's greater commitment to generous social programs. Within Europe, advocates of budgetary austerity for Greece, Italy, Spain, Ireland, and other nations forced to pay high interest rates on their government bonds also draw on a version of the Eurosclerosis argument. They insist that without significant cutbacks in entitlement programs, government budgets will not return to balance, and that will continue to discourage the new investments by the private sector that are critical for the restoration of growth.

Such arguments are deeply ironic; it has been the European nations that are laggards in public provision, whose programs and benefits are considerably less generous, that have been having the greatest difficulties in the post-2008 period. The nations with the most generous programs of public provision, particularly the Nordic nations and Germany, have experienced relatively vigorous employment growth and have not been the focus of the Eurocrisis.[14] This fact alone would suggest that there is something very wrong with the claim that protecting citizens against the risks of illness, unemployment, and old age is somehow incompatible with the success of a market system.

The key problem with such arguments is that public provision plays a huge role in making a nation's labor force more productive. The very large investments that the United States made in educating its labor force both in the nineteenth century and through much of the twentieth century were extremely important for making the U.S. the world's most productive economy. And today, despite the competition from cheap labor in Asia, countries of Northern Europe such as Germany and the Scandinavian countries continue to be extremely effective in exporting sophisticated manufactured goods and advanced services. They are able to do this because they now have the world's healthiest and most literate labor forces, workers who are able to meet the challenges of twenty-first-century production.[15]

The U.S., in contrast, has been struggling in recent years in the international marketplace. The reason for this is clear. Since the 1970s, the U.S. has retreated from its international leadership in investing in its labor force. While the U.S. had been far ahead of other nations in the percentage of young people who went on to college, retrenchment that began in the 1970s has meant that many other nations have caught up with and exceeded the U.S. in levels of educational attainment.[16] To be sure, the U.S. continues to be able to attract some of the best scientists and engineers from around the world as a way to maintain its innovation system, but this is not a good strategy for the long term. Countries such as China and India have had aggressive policies to attract these people back to their homeland, and other nations are likely to follow. If this happens, the U.S. will lack the trained technologists needed to make its innovation system work.

CONCLUSION

The conventional wisdom is that democracy is a threat to a market society's economic vitality. The danger is that self-interested politicians win office by promising the public more than the society can afford; the result is meddlesome government that hamstrings business and enacts expensive entitlement programs that either drive tax rates through the roof or threaten governmental bankruptcy. But this is a tendentious and inaccurate reading of history; the reality is exactly the opposite.

Before the emergence of modern democracies with widespread political rights, wealthy elites simply appropriated most of the society's wealth for themselves. They used their control over government to consolidate their entrenched position and eliminate any economic or political challengers. These elites sometimes invested in improved production processes or in a better infrastructure of roads and canals, but the rates of new investment were not high enough to produce the kind of sustained economic growth that has occurred in some countries over the last two centuries.

The kind of sustained growth that has characterized the United States for the last century and a half has been deeply dependent on democratic institutions. First, democracy has allowed the electorate to place limits on the capacity of economic elites to command a disproportionate share of resources, creating an economy that is pushed along by mass consumption. Second, democracy has consistently created openings for upstart firms that are able to transform industries by introducing new products and new processes. Third, democratic deliberation has led to huge public-sector infrastructure investments that drive the economy forward. Finally, democratic politics has won forms of state spending on education, income security, and health care that improve the quality of life for many people. These quality improvements, in turn, help create a more productive population that is able to sustain continuing productivity advances.

However, highly influential free market thinkers have argued over the last forty years that the path to economic renewal in the United States requires protecting the market economy from democratic politics. They have favored putting up barriers to keep government from imposing new regulations on business, they have argued for limiting the ability of legislatures to raise taxes or approve unbalanced budgets, and they have campaigned relentlessly to roll back "entitlement spending" that they claim the society cannot afford. And, of course, they have persuaded the U.S. Supreme Court to pass a series of rulings that allow the wealthy to exert disproportionate influence on election outcomes through their campaign donations.

These efforts have produced significant results.[17] As we have learned from the research of Thomas Piketty and others, the share of income and wealth going to the top 1 percent of households has increased precipitously.[18] And a handful of ultra-wealthy oligarchs have increasing influence over our politics. But the results have not included the promised renewal of the U.S. economy.

On virtually every measure, the performance of the U.S. economy has been worse over the thirty-five years since Ronald Reagan's election in 1980 than it had been in the three decades after World War II. And it is increasingly clear that this poor performance is linked to the power of giant firms that dominate sector after sector of the U.S. economy. This dominance is obvious in finance, where the too-big-to-fail firms have become even larger since the 2008 crisis. The internet is now dominated by Amazon, Apple, Facebook, Google, and Microsoft. A handful of giant communications and entertainment firms exert enormous control over the production and dissemination of cultural content. Similar patterns exist with pharmaceuticals, food and beverages, and defense industries.[19] This economic concentration has pushed the U.S. closer to an oligarchic economy.

The irony is that the belief in an autonomous and self-regulating economy has helped create an economy that is increasingly stagnant and unproductive. The actual path to economic renewal in the United States is to strengthen democracy—to give the public greater influence over key economic decisions. This has been the mechanism throughout history that has created dynamic and strong market economies.

CHAPTER FOUR

The Illusion That Greed Is Good

Another illusion is the belief that the economy will work best when people pursue their self-interest without restraint. Since the market's ability to allocate resources depends on price signals, it is imperative that people hear those signals and respond to them. For this reason, everyone needs to be a maximizer who is undeterred by such considerations as friendship, patriotism, or a desire for eternal salvation. All other values are essentially noise that might lead us to pay insufficient attention to the important signals that the market is constantly sending. Like an engineer who is distracted as the train goes through a dangerous intersection, the economic actor who fails to respond to signals can produce horrible consequences.

The great theorist of the free market, Milton Friedman, expressed this logic in the argument he made against corporate social responsibility.[1] He argued that the corporation's only responsibility was to maximize profits because that imperative focused the corporation on price signals, and the rapid adjustment to price signals is the way that the market system assures the optimal use of all resources. If corporations were to suddenly develop a conscience, signals would be missed and resources would be used suboptimally; ultimately everyone would suffer from a less productive economy.

Friedman was certainly aware of one obvious flaw in his logic. He and his Chicago colleagues knew well that firms can make profits by imposing "externalities," or public bads, on others. Environmental degradation is the classic instance of a public bad that is produced as individuals or firms respond to market signals. In the absence of regulations that prohibit such practices, the signals of the price system incentivize firms to maximize the output of these public bads because a firm can make greater profits if it disregards the health and safety of its workforce or pours toxic effluents into nearby rivers. The minute one remembers the existence of externalities, Friedman's argument completely loses its force, since firms that embrace social responsibility would be likely to reduce the production of public bads, and that alone would improve how the market system deploys resources.

A second flaw in Friedman's logic extends to an even broader range of transactions. Friedman and his allies consistently exaggerate the effectiveness of markets as information processing machines. The reality is that in most market situations, consumers lack key pieces of information for rational decision making. For example, most people don't know whether the car actually needs a new muffler or a new transmission when they take it to the mechanic. When they buy a pint of strawberries, they don't know if the ones on the bottom have already gotten moldy. Even in economic theory, price signals will not optimize the use of resources when consumers are being misled about what they are getting for their dollars. This is precisely why in building economic models, economists frequently posit perfect information.

By simply assuming that everybody has all the relevant information, they can assure that the model produces optimal outcomes. But in the actual world, there are very few situations in which both buyers and sellers have perfect information.[2] Friedman systematically ignores this problem in making arguments against government regulation.

In their widely read popularization of free market ideas, *Free to Choose*, Milton and Rose Friedman are explicit that all forms of government regulation are an undesirable restriction on individual freedom: "Today you are not free to offer your services as a lawyer, a physician, a dentist, a plumber, a barber, a mortician, or engage in a host of other occupations, without first getting a permit or a license from a government official."[3] The implication is clear; real freedom means that anybody should be able to put out a shingle indicating that he or she is providing medical services, and presumably the world would beat a path to the doors of those practitioners with the higher levels of skill. The Friedmans fail to acknowledge that medical licensing arose precisely because it was so difficult for consumers to tell the difference between good doctors and quacks.

This issue, however, goes far beyond the polemical strategies of Friedman and other free market theorists. The intellectual error is parallel to that related to thinking that democracy undermines economic efficiency. The reality is that restraining the individual's pursuit of self-interest is, in fact, necessary for a well-functioning economy. A deeply rooted critique of selfishness and acquisitiveness is part of what has made market economies successful in those places where they have flourished. The endless stream of Sunday morning sermons warning the congregation against pride, greed, and excessive materialism have not been obstacles to an effective market economy; they helped to make it work.

This paradox helps to explain the enduring significance of a literary classic from 1843. In both England and the United States, the two countries where the rhetoric of maximizing profits has been most deeply influential, people return each holiday season to Charles Dickens's scathing critique of greed and selfishness in *A Christmas Carol.* The figure of Ebenezer Scrooge does important cultural work in explaining to each new generation the dangers of fully internalizing the values of the market. Even Walt Disney, not known as a critic of capitalism, embraced the same logic by making Scrooge McDuck, Donald's plutocratic uncle, part of the Disney pantheon.

This dependence of the market system on the rejection of unbridled greed and selfishness has been understood by social theorists back to Adam Smith. Some of these theorists have worried that society might not be able to hold on to a constructive equilibrium between self-interest and other-regarding behaviors. The concern is that as people are constantly bombarded by market signals and market propaganda, they will embrace the pursuit of self-interest without reservation and this could undermine the economy. In fact, the dominance of free market ideas in the U.S. over the last thirty-five years has created just this kind of deep cultural confusion and economic dysfunction.

FROM ADAM SMITH TO THE SOCIOLOGICAL TRADITION

Adam Smith, the author of *The Wealth of Nations,* has often been proclaimed as the patron saint of the free market. But Smith's earlier book, *The Theory of Moral Sentiments* (hereafter TMS), is almost always ignored by market liberals; they either ignore it entirely or say that it reflected a sensibility that Smith later outgrew. But most serious Smith scholars see the two books as closely connected and as sharing the same set of philosophical premises.

This is important because in TMS, Smith argues that a shared morality is required for social order, and he cautions against an excess of greed, ambition, or vanity.

> Avarice over-rates the difference between poverty and riches: ambition, that between a private and a public station: vain-glory, that between obscurity and extensive reputation. The person under the influence of any of those extravagant passions, is not only miserable in his actual situation, but is often disposed to disturb the peace of society, in order to arrive at that which he so foolishly admires. The slightest observation, however, might satisfy him, that, in all the ordinary situations of human life, a well-disposed mind may be equally calm, equally cheerful, and equally contented.[4]

By a well-disposed mind, Smith clearly means one that has placed limits on the strivings of the ego. Elsewhere in the book, he emphasizes the importance of competitors observing the rules of the game in order to avoid earning society's disdain:

> In the race for wealth, honours, and promotions he may run as hard as he can, straining every nerve and muscle in order to outstrip all his competitors. But if he should jostle or trip any of them, the allowance of the spectators is entirely at an end—that is a violation of fair play that they can't allow.... They now sympathize with the natural resentment of the person who was shouldered aside or tripped, and the offender becomes an object of their hatred and indignation. He is aware of this, and feels that those sentiments are ready to burst out from all sides against him.[5]

Similar sentiments appear in *The Wealth of Nations*, as when Smith writes that "people of the same trade seldom meet together, even for merriment and diversion, but the conversation ends in a conspiracy against the public, or in some contrivance to raise prices."[6] All this suggests that Smith did not actually imagine that the market economy was a self-regulating system. On the contrary, he saw it as depending on a shared moral order and the enforcement of legal rules to prevent the pursuit of self-interest from spinning out of control. His defense of self-interest, in short, assumed the existence of moral constraints. If in the race for competitive advantage actors were allowed to routinely commit fouls such as tripping and pushing, Smith would not have confidently asserted that we owe our dinners to the self-interest of the butcher, the brewer, or the baker.

Smith's recognition that a market economy depends on anti-market values was replicated by such key sociological thinkers as Émile Durkheim and Max Weber. Durkheim, writing in the last decades of the nineteenth century, was responding to Herbert Spencer's insistence that freely contracted exchanges were sufficient to create a well-ordered society. Durkheim noted the inherent complexity of the situation of those who would enter a contract: "The conditions for their cooperation must also be fixed for the entire duration of their relationship. The duties and rights of each one must be defined, not only in the light of the situation as it presents itself at the moment when the contract is concluded, but in anticipation of circumstances that can arise and can modify it. Otherwise, at every moment there would be renewed conflicts and quarrels."[7] Durkheim argued that both the law of contracts and a shared morality were necessary to prevent the constant renewal of conflicts and quarrels. In short, the order that Spencer was talking about came not from private contracting but from the noncontractual bases of contract provided by morality and law. Yet Durkheim also worried that social solidarity was being undermined by the pursuit of individual self-interest, and this was the basis of his argument in favor of a system of occupational assemblies that would elaborate distinct codes of conduct for each occupation and make people more aware of their mutual interdependence.

Max Weber, writing in the first decades of the twentieth century, was convinced that definitions of capitalism that focused on the pursuit of profit were not adequate or accurate. He made a distinction between "adventurers' capitalism" and "rational capitalism," which was his name for the dominant system of his time. Both types of capitalism featured a relentless pursuit of profit, but adventurers such as pirates and explorers did not engage in the reinvestment of profits and the ongoing improvement of production processes that Weber considered the hallmarks of rational capitalism.[8]

For Weber, this distinction between adventurers' capitalism and rational capitalism suggested a historical puzzle. While greed alone could explain the emergence of adventurers' capitalism, it could not explain the origins of rational capitalism because the founders of rational capitalism needed to defer gratification by reinvesting their profits for years at a time. Weber's solution was to argue that the first several generations of rational capitalists were Calvinists who were preoccupied not with material gain but with eternal salvation. Their religious commitments required that they avoid idleness and ostentation, and this, in turn, facilitated the disciplined hard work and the reinvestment of profits that created the first modern business fortunes.[9]

The issue here is not the historical accuracy of Weber's account. Rather, it is that Weber recognized the hybridity of the value system on which modern economies were built. In his view, the modern economy had been created by combining the pursuit of material gains with a powerful critique of materialism as dangerous and sinful. However, Weber shared Durkheim's anxiety that the passage of time was eroding values that placed limits on the individual pursuit of self-interest.

Weber's concerns were taken up by the U.S. sociologist Daniel Bell in the 1970s in *The Cultural Contradictions of Capitalism*.[10] Bell argued that from the side of production, the modern economy requires a work ethic that prioritizes self-discipline and personal sacrifice. However, with the rise of mass production in the 1920s, the economy also needs mass consumption, which is engineered through an advertising industry that emphasizes pleasure and the immediate gratification of the senses. While these conflicting imperatives have existed in uneasy harmony for several generations, Bell worried that the tensions could no longer be contained, so that the drive for immediate gratification was finally undermining all that was left of the work ethic.

More recently, the sociologist Viviana Zelizer has proposed a more nuanced view of these same issues. Zelizer begins by arguing that the fear that profit maximizing would erode morality, trust, and meaningful human relationships has been present in Western societies since Shakespeare's time. Marx also expressed this fear in his early writings, particularly in his critique of money as a solvent of true values. This fear was elaborated in the early twentieth century by Georg Simmel, and later by scores of other social analysts. Zelizer takes comfort in the fact that the identical lament has been expressed every generation for at least four centuries.

Her alternative argument is that just as the pursuit of self-interest is continually being reinforced by our everyday experiences, so are values such as love, friendship, reciprocity, and honesty. We learn this alternative set of values in the family, in our friendships, and in our intimate relationships. Zelizer's argument, in effect, is that we all learn to be bilingual—to speak the language of self-interest in certain settings and to speak the very different language of reciprocity and deep personal commitments in other settings.[11] This bilingualism has been part of the human condition for generations now. Hence, Zelizer is confident that most of the time we do not get confused; when someone we care about asks us for a favor, we try not to say: "So, what's in it for me?"

Zelizer recognizes that one cannot actually survive in a market society without learning how to turn off the signals of the market. Think, for example, of the insistent advertising messages that we all receive thousands of times in any given day. If we actually believed the message that consuming this particular food or traveling to that exotic locale would actually make us happier, we would likely empty our bank accounts by the end of the week. But most of us have learned to be highly skeptical about those messages, and we teach our children that advertisers lie and that their products do not have the magical powers that are constantly being claimed.

But Zelizer's approach also allows room for the kinds of concerns that Durkheim expressed toward the end of the nineteenth century. Yes, we are all bilingual and we have the ability to switch almost effortlessly from the language of self-interest to the alternative language of friendship, love, and solidarity. One language does not obliterate the other. Our choices, though, are influenced by our immediate environment and especially the cultural values and legal rules within which we practice our bilingualism. It is in terms of this cultural and legal environment that we can see the impact of changes over the last few centuries.

When market societies first emerged, religion was still a powerful force, and Christianity provided a needed counterweight to the values of the market. But over the course of the nineteenth century, as Western societies experienced a process of secularization, it was the rise of socialism as a movement that gave other-regarding values a new grounding in social life. In fact, socialist movements adopted much of their moral vision from the Gospels in their emphasis on solidarity and the conviction that those at the bottom of society would experience redemption. In their secularized form, these values were very potent because of people's concrete experiences of solidarity at the workplace and in everyday life.

The data assembled by Thomas Piketty in his book *Capital in the Twenty-First Century* show clearly that from 1914 through the 1970s, the share of income and wealth going to the top 1 percent of households was at a historically low level in England, France, and the United States. Since this period includes what has been called the "golden age" of economic growth, from 1945 to 1975, it is not difficult to see that market societies experienced the greatest prosperity when socialist ideas exerted considerable counterforce against the value that greed is good.

But this history also suggests what has gone wrong in recent decades. Secularization has progressed in Europe and the U.S. to the point where religion no longer provides any kind of counterweight to self-interested behavior. While survey data shows continuing high rates of Christian belief in the U.S., many of the adherents have embraced the "prosperity gospel" of Evangelical churches that now celebrates, rather than criticizes, the pursuit of wealth. Moreover, since the fall of the Berlin Wall in 1989, neither communism nor socialism represents a real threat to the market system, and the values espoused by generations of socialists have lost their force. This is the context in which the deeply erroneous free market ideas of Milton Friedman and Friedrich

Hayek have taken on the character of a new religion that celebrates the unconstrained pursuit of self-interest.

THE CONFUSED PHARMACIST

An exemplary case can sometimes illustrate a broader set of issues. Back in 2002, Robert Courtney was a pharmacist practicing in Kansas City, Missouri, and a deacon in a local congregation of the Assembly of God, a Christian evangelical denomination.[12] He was charged in federal court with twenty counts of tampering with and adulterating chemotherapy drugs that he was providing to local oncologists for their patients. Since the drugs were very expensive, the dilution of doses allowed him to increase his earnings very significantly. He was not just cheating these victims financially; he could well have doomed them to earlier deaths by making their chemotherapy less effective. He pleaded guilty to the charges, and after his sentencing, he explained to the court that he needed the money because he had pledged $1 million to the building fund of his church.

This was obviously an individual who was bilingual in Zelizer's sense; he understood that very different imperatives governed the world of commerce compared with those governing the world of eternal values. And yet, he was also obviously deeply confused about Christian teachings, especially the commandment not to steal. While he might simply have been a deranged individual whose case has no broader significance, I see him as symptomatic of a broader set of problems.

My hypothesis is that Courtney was influenced by prevailing economic ideas and particularly the celebration of the pursuit of self-interest in the marketplace. Imagine that he agreed with Friedman's argument that the only responsibility of a business is to maximize profits. In other words, he saw no connection between the realm of business activity and the realm of religious obligation. He interpreted "render unto Caesar" to mean that all is fair in the struggle to make a profit, and the test of whether one is obeying God's law concerns only one's behavior in relationships outside of the market. Such a belief makes sense if it is assumed that the invisible hand of the market will produce optimal results even when those racing to earn profits shove their competitors or their customers to the ground.

To be sure, Friedman and other free market economists have not counseled their readers to lie, cheat, or steal, much less kill. (Ayn Rand, however, certainly suggests that ruthlessness is appropriate in the marketplace.)[13] But their screeds against government regulation carry the message that market competition will be able to solve the problem of fraudulent acts if only regulators would get out of the way. The constant invoking of the "magic of the market" has given ordinary people the false and exaggerated sense that all is fair in war and market exchange. Is it any wonder that someone like Courtney became confused about what were and were not legitimate ways to earn the money needed for the church building fund?

While Courtney's crime is particularly gruesome, we have had in the last twenty years many examples of seemingly decent businesspeople who have violated almost every rule in the book in their quest for greater profits. Think of those involved in cooking the books at Enron and WorldCom or those upstanding investment bankers who cheerfully sold mortgage bonds based on extremely dubious subprime loans while traders at their banks were betting that those same bonds were going to lose their value because of rising loan defaults. And the thousands of mortgage brokers who engaged in predatory transactions with people living in inner-city neighborhoods who led countless borrowers to lose homes they had lived in for many years. More recently, dozens of high-level banking officials were caught artificially manipulating interest rates and the markets for foreign exchange. Even if one puts to one side the sociopaths, like the Ponzi financier Bernard Madoff, examples abound of similar behavior in those who were respected members of their communities and who professed to be deeply committed to one or another religious faith.[14] Numbers alone suggest that there is something going on besides individual pathology.

Aside from the sheer numbers of such cases, consider the political rise of Donald Trump, an avatar of the idea that the pursuit of self-interest represents the noblest calling. During the presidential campaign, whenever his business tactics were questioned, Trump would defend himself by arguing that it was his responsibility as a businessperson to be as aggressive as possible in pursuing his self-interest. As a businessperson, he asserted, he is obligated to go right up to the line separating legal and illegal behavior. Trump also campaigned vigorously for dismantling much of the structure of government regulation of business because it was discouraging entrepreneurial initiatives. But without regulations and regulators, the line between legal and illegal behavior would cease to exist. He was never forced to explain how this combination of aggressive businesses and minimal regulation could possibly produce benign outcomes.

The emergence of an openly anti-authoritarian business culture has also contributed to the "greed-is-good" ethos. The rise of the computer industry in Silicon Valley created a new kind of business subculture that was exemplified by the famous Apple "big brother" television advertisement in which IBM was associated with an Orwellian system of control against which Apple was organizing resistance. This new business subculture worships the disruption of established practices and values. This shift was addressed by *New York Times* columnist David Brooks in his book *Bobos in Paradise*.[15] Brooks's Bobos are bourgeois bohemians; they represent a strange amalgam of the values held by what had long been deeply antagonistic cultures. Bobos join the systematic pursuit of profits with the anti-authoritarianism and the "do-your-own-thing" ethic of the counterculture of the 1970s. Many Bobos gravitate toward libertarianism because it combines liberalism on social issues such as drug laws and homosexuality with a deep faith that unfettered markets will produce both freedom and prosperity. In the 1990s especially, Bobo libertarianism as expressed by *Wired* magazine was extremely influential among both computer engineers and entrepreneurs in Silicon Valley.

In articulating its libertarian vision, *Wired* drew heavily on the writings of Friedrich Hayek, the Austrian economist who envisioned the market as a system that produced a spontaneous order out of the conflicting intentions of different actors. Any subtleties in Hayek's actual writings were forgotten; all government actions were destructive and counterproductive, and the market mechanism had an almost supernatural capacity to turn selfish individual behavior into outcomes that were optimal for all. Hence, entrepreneurs were most productive when they disrupted older ways of doing things, including those dictated by now-obsolete moral codes.

While the influence of these ideas in Silicon Valley is well known, it is less widely recognized that Bobo values and politics migrated to the financial markets in that same decade.[16] The key mechanism of transfer was the increasingly important role of sophisticated information processing in generating Wall Street profits. There was a flood of so-called rocket scientists into financial firms who helped design and manage both computer-driven trading schemes and the use of increasingly complex financial instruments. Many of these newcomers brought with them the distrust of authority and preference for disruption that was part of the Bobo ethic. These ideas spread rapidly among the new cohorts of young people who flooded into Wall Street firms in the first decade of the twenty-first century.

The 2013 movie *The Wolf of Wall Street* depicts the lower-status end of Wall Street, where cheap stocks are sold through boiler room tactics; but some of the same sex- and drug-fueled get-rich-quick culture reached into Goldman Sachs and other elite firms. This meant that brokers and traders did not just succumb to the temptation to cheat because they were pressured by their bosses to produce bigger profits. Rather, many of them were empowered by an ideology claiming that their ruthless and disruptive pursuit of self-interest would make everybody in the society better off because of the magic of markets.

THE FAILURE OF THE JUDICIAL SYSTEM

The problematic ethics of Bobo libertarians would not be such a serious issue but for changes in how our judicial system handles the transgressions of businesspeople. This is the result of a judicial counterrevolution, also inspired by free market theorists, that has unfolded over the last generation. The consequence is that society's last defense against runaway greed has been crippled. Even where the political will to prosecute white-collar criminals is present, obtaining a conviction has become exceedingly difficult because prosecutors must now prove not only that the behavior was unethical and predatory, but that the defendants willfully intended to hurt their victims.[17] To avoid a conviction, all that a good CEO has to do is to avoid leaving any traces in email or oral messages that he or she actively wanted to cause others harm. This is not difficult; all they have to do is tell their subordinates to do whatever needs to be done to boost the bottom line. If they don't also say, "And break any law you have to," they are pretty much safe.

Much of this has happened because ideas that were shared by much of the legal community in the 1930s and 1940s have either been forgotten or deliberately repressed over the last three or four decades. In the early part of the twentieth century, the federal judiciary was dominated by rigid adherence to free market doctrine. In the infamous Lochner decision (1905), the Supreme Court ruled that New York State legislation that placed limits on the workday of bakers represented an illegitimate interference in the right of parties to contract freely. This doctrine erected an enormous barrier against efforts at both the state and the federal level to reform and regulate markets.

To challenge the Lochner barrier, legal thinkers engaged in a serious effort to understand more clearly what the "freedom of contract" did and did not entail. The cutting edge of this initiative was the work of thinkers who are grouped under the rubric of legal realism. Some of the legal realists, influenced by institutional economists such as Thorstein Veblen and John Commons, came to the insight that actual market relations differ considerably from the idealized markets of economic theory, where perfect information is assumed. In actual markets, there is a power struggle between buyers and sellers, lenders and borrowers, landlords and tenants, and the relative power of these parties influences the price and specific terms of the contract between them.[18]

This insight provided much of the justification for the regulatory initiatives of Franklin Roosevelt's New Deal. Whether the regulations concerned financial markets, labor markets, anti-trust, or energy markets, the basic logic was the same. At the end of the day, there was to be a contract between two parties who agreed to do business at a particular price and with particular terms. But through the regulatory scheme, the government was attempting to diminish the power differential between the two parties, so that the terms more closely resembled what would have happened had the parties been equal and had complete information. In this way, regulation could move the economy closer to prices that did, in fact, optimize the use of resources.

This view of markets as arenas in which power struggles take place came to be shared by regulators and judges, and it undergirded the thirty years of prosperity after World War II. However, at the end of the 1960s, the rise of consumer and environmental movements created strong pressures for a further extension of government regulation. Corporate leaders felt embattled and recognized that the understandings that had been carried over from the 1930s provided them with little leverage to resist a further expansion in the reach of the government's regulatory efforts. This is when they took a right turn and embraced the ideas of free market economists such as Milton Friedman and his Chicago allies.

Through a legal movement called "law and economics," a counterattack was launched that challenged the tradition represented by the legal realists.[19] Instead of focusing on the conflicted exchanges on actual markets, the law and economics analysts relied almost entirely on economic theory. The approach was to begin with the actions of regulators that were intended to make markets work more effectively. Evidence was mobilized to show that these regulatory efforts were not producing the desired outcome. Instead of suggesting a way to fine-tune the regulatory process, they would assert that the regulatory effort was undermining the price signals of the marketplace. The last step was to invoke economic theory to "prove" that if the market were left alone, it would produce the desired outcome. The conclusion was almost always the same; things would be better if we dismantled the regulatory apparatus and let the market work autonomously.

These legal theorists also responded to the concerns of the business community by arguing that ordinary business decisions should not be criminalized. Executives and managers should be allowed to go about the business of maximizing profits without worrying whether a bad decision might get them thrown in jail. Here again, they had to ignore the legal realist view of market transactions as power struggles. Corporate managers were simply doing their job of maximizing profits, and if they inadvertently crossed a particular legal line, it was not a criminal offense since they lacked criminal intent. Criminal penalties should apply only to those situations where there was a clear intent to violate the law.

While this position sounds reasonable, it ignores the point that Adam Smith made so clearly in *The Theory of Moral Sentiments* that participants in a competition have to obey the rules of the game because results are far from optimal when participants trip or jostle their opponents. Or, as Durkheim put it, part of the noncontractual basis of contracts is that both parties are operating in good faith, so that what they say during the process of negotiation can be trusted. It follows that for these markets to work optimally, the courts must question contracts where one party has systematically misrepresented the facts, and those who have made such misrepresentations should face criminal prosecution for fraud.

In other words, establishing a certain ethical floor for business transactions is not criminalizing ordinary business behavior.

Rather, it is necessary to maintain the moral constraints on which a market system depends. Nor would such an approach promise a vast increase in litigation or criminal prosecutions. As with other violations, creating a legally enforced ethical floor would send a signal to market participants that various deceptive practices that had earlier been tolerated will no longer be permitted. Since few people want to go to jail, it is likely that establishing this norm would actually change behavior. Our experience with creating penalties for discrimination on racial or gender lines demonstrates that legal enforcement can change behavior. Open forms of racial and gender bias are far less prevalent at the workplace than they were a generation ago.

The idea here is that we would treat those doing business in the same way that we treat professionals such as doctors, lawyers, and accountants. Members of those professions are required to maintain a certain ethical standard in their interactions, and they can be held liable for breaches of their professional obligations. Think, for example, of the case of a surgeon who had a few drinks before performing an operation and then completed the procedure with surgical instruments sewn up in the patient's abdomen. In mounting a defense, the surgeon's intention to harm the patient would not be a relevant consideration. The violation of ethical norms would be enough to make the physician vulnerable to a malpractice suit and possibly even criminal charges.

With this standard in mind, the legal treatment of Angelo Mozilo, the former CEO of Countrywide Financial, would have been very different from what actually happened. Countrywide Financial was one of the largest mortgage brokers in the country. The firm used all of the techniques of modern corporate management to maximize the number of predatory loans to inner-city minority homeowners in the years leading up to the financial crisis, with full knowledge that most of its borrowers would ultimately lose their homes. This activity did not just hurt minority homeowners; it played a key role in the collapse of major banks because the ultimate default rate on those mortgages was so high. Mozilo made hundreds of millions of dollars from this activity, but he successfully avoided any criminal prosecution. He was forced to pay a fine of $67.5 million to the Securities and Exchange Commission in October 2012, but he was still left with a huge fortune. More importantly, the signal to others is that if one carries out criminal activity on a large enough scale, there will be no penalty.[20]

But if we assume a legal regime in which the CEOs of all firms that passed a certain size threshold were treated as business professionals who had to complete trainings in business ethics, the outcome would have been different. Mozilo's expensive legal team and his careful avoidance of sending emails that counseled subordinates to engage in illegal behavior would not have been sufficient as an effective defense against prosecution. The U.S. attorney would simply have to provide evidence that Mozilo's subordinates had systematically and routinely engaged in fraudulent activity. A CEO who had failed to monitor these subordinates and prevented them from engaging in these types of behavior would be criminally liable for a breach of his professional duty to run an organization that remained on the proper side of the law.

ENCOURAGING PREDATION

There is a deeper irony here. We have seen that the defenders of the modern market system grabbed the term "capitalism" from the left and have celebrated it as being the world's most productive way to organize an economy. They have extolled the magic of autonomous markets that require individuals to be self-interested maximizers, and they have persuaded the court system that businesspeople must have broad discretion to respond aggressively when they see business opportunities. However, they have opened the door wide to predatory business practices that are actually economically unproductive. In fact, the more money that businesses can make by cheating, the less likely they are to invest in expanding productivity. So in the name of economic efficiency, free market theorists have tilted our economy in an increasingly unproductive direction.

We have seen that there are two divergent strategies by which firms can make profits. They can impose costs on others or they can improve the efficiency with which goods and services are produced. One form of cost shifting is to gain government protection that insulates a firm from the threat of competition. The other type of cost shifting is literally taking from others by forcing them to accept an unequal exchange. Such takings include imposing heavy environmental costs on a neighborhood or on nature, forcing employees to accept substandard wages and working conditions, and tricking people into accepting predatory home loans. All of these are basically easier ways to earn a profit than figuring out how to make continuous improvements in the goods and services one is producing.

In the last chapter, we saw that free market policies clear the way for an oligarchic and unproductive "crony capitalism" by giving entrenched firms more opportunities to get government to do their bidding. But those same free market ideas and policies also create increased opportunities for firms to focus their energies on seeking profits through predation. In recent years, we have seen case after case of business firms that have pursued such "low road" business strategies as engaging in systematic "wage theft" from their employees, lying to the public about climate change to justify continued government policies in support of burning coal and oil, selling pharmaceuticals with dangerous side effects, and colluding among themselves to raise prices.

But perhaps the most egregious example is a practice that has become widespread among high-level corporate executives. This is the systematic use of share repurchases as a corporate governance strategy. The history of this goes back to the 1970s, when it became clear that many big U.S. corporations were losing market share to Japanese and European competitors. Many analysts reached the conclusion that large U.S. corporations had become complacent and badly managed, focusing on growth rather than increasing efficiency or profitability. While different solutions were proposed at the time, the one that prevailed was an idea pushed by market-oriented economists. They argued that if compensation schemes aligned the interests of top managers with those of shareholders, then those managers would prioritize increasing efficiency and profitability.[21]

Their tool of choice for accomplishing alignment was to make top managers into shareholders, so they would profit directly when the firms' share price increased. Stock grants and stock options became a key element in executive compensation over the next three decades. During this same period, executive compensation rose dramatically relative to the pay of rank-and-file employees. These big increases in executive compensation can be traced directly to the value of stock grants and stock options and related mechanisms.

To be sure, there is little evidence to date that this form of alignment has, in fact, improved corporate governance. On the contrary, evidence indicates that the resulting relentless pursuit of "shareholder value" by top managers has focused them on improving short-term results even if this is problematic for the firm over the longer term. We have seen, for example, many firms cut back on expenditures for research laboratories because those efforts cannot be expected to bear fruit quickly enough to impact the firm's share value.

But what has made matters considerably worse is that managers came to recognize that stock repurchases could be used in tandem with stock options and stock grants to increase their own compensation. As recently as 1980, such share repurchases were trivial, but in the twenty-first century, they have reached the level of $300 to $500 billion per year. Increasingly, rather than returning profits to shareholders through dividends, firms return the profits by buying back shares. There are also numerous cases in which firms borrow funds that are then used to finance share repurchases.[22]

The essential logic is that by reducing the number of outstanding shares, the repurchases improve the firm's earnings per share even if actual sales or profits are flat. This has become a mechanism that allows top managers to appear to be improving the firm's bottom line whether or not their decisions have actually produced better results. But by timing the share repurchases to fit with the granting of their own stock options, these same managers are able to maximize their personal returns, taking them as capital gains, which are taxed at lower rates than salary income. This is how the share of corporate earnings that go directly into the pockets of a handful of top managers has risen dramatically, and this, in turn, is one of the main reasons that the top 1 percent of households have dramatically increased their fraction of total income.

But this is an arrangement that makes no actual economic sense. It is a tails, I win, heads, you lose proposition in which incumbent executives gain regardless of their effectiveness as managers. It is not just that this compensation system fails to incentivize managers to be effective; it has toxic consequences throughout the whole organization. The huge gap in compensation between CEOs and ordinary employees reduces morale and reinforces the cynical view that the firm is just an enrichment scheme for a tiny group of people. Moreover, the enormous gains of reaching the top encourage total ruthlessness in plotting one's way to the executive suite. The consequence is a distortion of decision making all through the organization, since the ambitious have incentives to prioritize personal advancement over the actual needs of the organization. These shortcomings in the steeply hierarchical structure of U.S. corporations were already well understood by the 1980s; the restructuring of executive compensation only made the situation worse.

THE MICRO-FOUNDATION MISUNDERSTANDING

A further problem is that proponents of maximal market freedom have advanced a widely accepted theory of causality in which the structure of the entire society is believed to be shaped by the actions of individuals responding to market signals. This view is encapsulated in the maxim of free market theorists that correctly defining the property rights in a given society will optimize the chances for prosperity and freedom.[23] This particular illusion has two disastrous consequences. First, it obscures the reality of class power; it renders invisible the role in society of those who control a disproportionate share of economic resources. Second, it diverts attention from the global rules and institutions that are often responsible for some of the market economy's most negative consequences, such as inequality, environmental destruction, and strict limits on what governments are allowed to do.

The history of this illusion can be traced back to the strategies that free market economists used in their long campaign to discredit and defeat Keynesian economics. They insisted that the theory developed by Keynesians lacked solid "micro-foundations." This meant that Keynesian economists could not explain how the choices made by individual economic actors produced the aggregate economic outcomes that Keynesian policies were designed to fix. Free market economists maintained that any compelling account of how an economy works must be rooted in explanations derived from the actions of individuals.

At first glance, this insistence on micro-foundations would seem to be in tension with the move made by Irving Kristol (described in chapter 1) to stand Karl Marx on his head. Kristol imported the Marxist idea of a capitalist system into conservative thought as a way to bolster the case that policies that violated the logic of capitalism as a system would inevitably make everyone poorer. In place of individual choice, Kristol emphasized that the structural logic of capitalism must be obeyed.

However, the tension here is only apparent. Kristol retained Milton Friedman's core idea that the beauty of capitalism is that individuals are "free to choose" what they want in response to the signals of the marketplace. It follows that once the proper system of contracts and property rights is in place, people are able to freely contract to meet their needs. Everything is driven by individual action, but in the aggregate, the result is a system with a unified and coherent logic. That coherent logic means that redistributive and regulatory policies will inevitably produce perverse outcomes.[24]

In short, causality works from the bottom up. Free and rational individuals make choices and this produces a uniquely productive system. Yes, there are constraints at the level of the resulting system, and political liberals routinely conspire to violate those constraints. But what political liberals fail to recognize is that those constraints are the outcome of freely chosen actions of individuals once the appropriate property rights have been put in place.

This theory of causality resonates with deep currents of individualism in the culture of the United States. It affirms the widespread belief that the individual is and should be sovereign; whether in religion or politics or economics, the individual needs to be the ultimate decider.[25] Even small children insist to each other that they cannot be made to do things that they don't want to do because this is "a free country."

While this approach to causality affirms the individual, it also deprives people of any actual agency to change things that really matter. For example, if someone does not like the wages being offered for unskilled work, there is not much that can be done about it. Forming a union or pushing to increase the legally mandated minimum wage hampers the ability of markets to balance supply and demand. Similarly, a consumer who believes that burning fossil fuels is endangering the planet can turn the thermostat down and even invest in solar panels, but taxing carbon represents an inappropriate effort to override the logic of capitalism.

Most importantly, this bottom-up theory of causality renders power and the workings of institutions invisible. If individuals are sovereign, there is no need to worry about the power exercised by the wealthy or by global institutions such as the International Monetary Fund or the World Bank. They are simply instruments of a capitalist order; they have no independent power or authority. This is obviously a convenient theory for those with power since it appears that they have no choice but to leave existing arrangements as they are. However, when those with power become captive of this illusion—when they believe vehemently in the absolute autonomy of markets—they may do nothing even when faced with obvious problems because they earnestly believe that they cannot "intervene" without causing further harm.

To dispel this particular illusion, we have to start with the problematic concept of micro-foundations. It is certainly true that anything that happens in a society ultimately depends upon the actions of individuals; in war, for example, individual soldiers must fire their weapons. But all actions taken by individuals are not the result of the free exercise of choice; individual acts are shaped by factors outside the individual, such as social structures, power relations, and culture. Someone who takes a poorly paid job with an abusive employer does so not out of free choice but because the alternatives are worse.

The micro-foundations approach fails to recognize the reality that individual actions occur within institutions such as business firms and political systems, and those institutions distribute power unevenly. It also ignores the reality of class power. In the previous chapter, I stressed that all societies are shaped by the power of people who own a disproportionate share of society's productive resources. This exercise of class power at the national level is also enhanced or diminished by the rules and institutions governing the global economy. Rather than the bottom-up causality of micro-foundations, I want to stress a top-down theory of causality that recognizes the central importance of the global level of institutions and rules.

This top-down approach acknowledges that the control of key economic resources within societies constrains the choices available to the rest of the population. But the degree to which wealth holders are able to dominate society varies over time and depends on the strength or weakness of democratic institutions. As I argued earlier, the great virtue of democracy is that it can constrain oligarchic power and force the wealthy to accept higher levels of political and economic equality. However, this contestation within societies is embedded within global arrangements that have often worked to enhance the political and economic power of the wealthy. The micro-foundations approach renders the global level of analysis completely invisible. For that reason, we will return to the importance of the global level in chapter 6.

CONCLUSION

The idea that we live in a capitalist society—one that is necessarily dominated by the market and the pursuit of self-interest—has actually eroded our prosperity and kept us from understanding that restraints on greed have always been necessary to make market systems work. The historical evidence is overwhelming that societies have to channel and constrain the pursuit of wealth both by enforcing legal rules that block various forms of predation and by creating cultures that strongly discourage selfishness and greed.

The greatest historical irony is that market fundamentalists such as Friedman and Hayek so thoroughly misunderstood the system to which they were devoted. While they had philosophical and methodological disagreements, both Hayek and Friedman truly believed that if society made the market the dominant social institution and taught people to prioritize the pursuit of wealth, then people would respond rapidly to market signals and the economy would flourish. But in asserting this, they had to disregard Adam Smith's warnings to the contrary, and they also had to ignore the actual histories of market societies. They made the classic mistake of constructing a model of how the economy works and then mistaking that model for reality. But the weakening of moral, regulatory, and legal restraints on greed have disastrous consequences. Many people have become deeply confused about the ethical framework in which they make their day-to-day and hour-by-hour economic decisions. The consequence has been disruptive financial crises, continuing scandals in the banking industry, and the transformation of our major corporations into machines for enriching top executives.

Solving this problem is actually not that difficult. It does not require some new upsurge in religious belief to reaffirm that the Golden Rule is an imperative that must govern our economic transactions. It is more a question of getting people to connect the dots and understand the implications of being bilingual—knowing how to speak both the language of the market and alternative language of love and solidarity. For example, even today, telling someone that they are selfish is a grave insult. This is what we say to the people we care about when they have let us down by being thoughtless or for not being present when we need their support. But imagine what would happen if people began to think that the rich, as a group, are phenomenally selfish and threaten society by their relentless pursuit of ever greater wealth?

There is, in fact, reason to believe that large percentages of U.S. citizens could be persuaded to perceive many of those with great wealth as selfish and undeserving. Several well-executed surveys have found that the extent of wealth and income inequality that currently exists within U.S. society violates most people's sense of what is fair and appropriate.[26] While it has always been true that people in the U.S. have a fairly high tolerance for income inequality, the realities of inequality now far exceed what most people consider reasonable. This in itself represents an important opening for posing critical questions about the morality and the ethics of those seeking wealth.

But the idea here is not to demonize the very rich; that would almost certainly backfire. The idea is rather to recognize that restoring shared prosperity in the United States requires a renewed commitment to those values that we all learned in kindergarten—share, take turns, don't hit, and don't eat the art supplies. To make sharing and taking turns a reality requires that the rich place limits on their greed and selfishness. They have to accept certain restraints as part of the price of living in a good society, and these restraints include paying their fair share of taxes and conducting their business affairs within quite strict ethical and legal guidelines.

But all of this means that we have to get rid of the mistaken baggage that is now attached to the concept of capitalism, including the pernicious idea that we should all be rational economic maximizers. Nothing is more important than that people doing business constantly ask themselves, "Am I doing the right thing? Does my behavior meet certain ethical standards? Does failure to disclose certain relevant factors mean that I am taking unfair advantage of another person?" When those questions are not asked, we start down the road to an unproductive economy dominated by predation.

CHAPTER FIVE

The Illusion of an Unchanging System

The previous two chapters argued that the concept of capitalism is misleading because it suggests that an economy built around the pursuit of profit constitutes an autonomous and coherent entity. The reality is that market systems work best when they are hybrids in which markets are counterbalanced with democratic institutions and with values that limit greed. Without democratic institutions, economic elites simply turn to forms of predation that are not economically productive. In the same way, a profit-oriented system requires strong values to constrain runaway greed, which is economically destructive. It follows that the triumph of free market ideas since the early 1980s has undermined this dynamic hybridity and has made our economy less productive and more wasteful.

This chapter challenges another one of the key pieces of baggage that comes with the concept of capitalism. This is the idea that the core institutional structures of capitalist societies have been stable for several centuries. There is little agreement among scholars over when "modern capitalism" actually started; some trace it as far back as the sixteenth century, while others find its start in the nineteenth.[1] But there is unanimity that once it was established, its core institutions remained pretty much fixed.

This idea of continuity and stability is a strikingly improbable claim. For the sake of argument, we can say that capitalism existed in France, the United States, and England by 1830, even though many would suggest earlier starting points. When we compare these three societies in 1830 to where they are in 2017, the changes have been monumental. In 1830, for example, most people still made their living on farms, and in the U.S. many of those people were legally defined as other people's property— slaves. In France and England, voting rights were limited to property holders, and in all three countries, people had very few of the civil and political rights that we now take for granted, such as freedom of speech and freedom of assembly. The modern corporation owned by shareholders had not yet emerged and railroads were just getting started.

So what do people actually mean when they say that both in 1830 and 2017, these societies are properly defined as capitalist? They insist that the kind of work people do and the political arrangements are superficial factors. They argue that behind these surface appearances, there are less visible structures that are continuous over time that exert great influence over the direction in which these societies develop. This underlying structure is an economy in which people make profits by producing goods and services for sale on competitive markets. Analysts posit that this structure provides the unchanging heart of a capitalist order.

This view also emphasizes the dynamism that results from this unchanging heart of capitalism. The competition to generate profits on markets produces a series of transformations in what society produces and how it is produced, as well as major shifts in politics and culture. The paradox is that specific features of capitalist societies are constantly being revolutionized by new inventions and new technologies, but the underlying driving force behind these changes is itself constant and unchanging. So, yes, they would concede that the work that people do, the way they travel, and the way they communicate have all been transformed, but that only confirms the dynamic nature of capitalism.

This argument can be understood through the analogy with biology and the idea of a genetic code. The United States might appear to be very different in 1830, in 1930, and in 2017, but its genetic code is largely unchanged in the same way that all species of mammals share most of the same genetic material. By the same logic, all capitalist societies share much of the same DNA, even though there can be huge differences in what they might look like to an outside observer.

Biologists have, however, actually isolated DNA and mapped the genetic code of many different mammalian species. They have also identified some of the specific pathways through which the messages encoded in the DNA shape the development of the organism. Social scientists do not have any comparable set of discoveries; they simply assert the existence of this shared DNA of capitalism and claim that it exerts a powerful influence over the direction that all such societies will take. They are, in short, proposing a hypothesis that is not easy to prove or disprove. I think this hypothesis needs to be treated with great skepticism.

CRITIQUES OF ESSENTIALISM

In the eighteenth century, as Europeans were becoming increasingly aware of the diversity of human societies in different parts of the planet, thinkers began to create typologies that identified distinct kinds of societies. Some typologies were more complex, with five or six distinct types, while others had only three or four. Some placed those different types in an evolutionary schema in which societies progressed from more backward to more advanced stages. Not surprisingly, these European thinkers almost always placed their own societies at the highest level of evolution. During the nineteenth century, and especially after Darwin's elaboration of the theory of biological evolution, this way of thinking became the dominant approach to human diversity.

This was the context in which Marx elaborated his scheme, in which social organization went through a series of stages from primitive communism to slavery to feudalism to capitalism to socialism and finally to communism. Marx emphasized that at each of these stages except the final one, there were internal tensions that would push the society forward toward the next stage. But Marx was hardly alone in creating this kind of theory of history; many of his contemporaries elaborated comparable schemes with their own explanations of the dynamics that moved things forward from one stage to the next.

Early in the twentieth century, the intellectual tide turned against these developmental schemas. Critics challenged the value of theories in which modern institutions were seen as inherently superior to the forms of social organization found among non-Europeans. They also attacked the idea of linearity, or the existence of some master process that assured that everybody was moving along the same evolutionary trajectory. The view of history as a progressive process leading humanity to improvement was widely shared in the nineteenth century, but this way of thinking did not hold up well when faced with the barbarism unleashed in the twentieth century.

Much of the rejection of evolutionary schemes centered on the problem of essentialism. Essentialism is the explanatory principle at work when the complex reality of entire societies is attributed to one or another underlying or essential characteristic that is seen to be driving development. It is actually a very old explanatory method that sees the actions of a particular entity—whether it is a thing or a society—as being explained entirely by one or another of its internal characteristics. So, for example, the phlogiston theory of burning that was elaborated in the seventeenth century was a form of essentialism. The theory insisted that burning things contained phlogiston, and that the heat and light we associate with burning was simply the release of that fire-like element. The phlogiston theory was discarded when scientists recognized that burning resulted from a chemical reaction involving oxygen in the atmosphere.

As with the phlogiston theory, essentialist explanations ignore the environment in which a thing or a society is located. Hence, biologists who emphasize the importance of environment have long criticized other biologists for engaging in a kind of genetic essentialism in which everything is explained by the organism's genetic code. And, in fact, the initial discovery and mapping of the DNA molecule did shift the historic debate over the relative importance of nature versus nurture in favor of a kind of DNA reductionism or essentialism. More recently, however, scientists have come to see that DNA includes an elaborate set of switches that turn particular genes on or off, and that factors in the organism's environment can effectively flip those switches in one direction or the other. Nature and nurture work in conjunction, which means that genetic essentialism is inherently incomplete;

organisms have been preprogrammed to respond differently to different kinds of environments.

But if biological essentialism is problematic, then the belief that an entire society's development is determined by a particular set of economic arrangements is even more suspect. The problems go beyond this essentialist logic, though. There is also the assumption that economic factors are always the most important in shaping a particular society. How do we know that politics or military power or ideologies might not at times override economics as the most important determinant of what shapes a society's particular path? In this respect, economic essentialism relies on an old-fashioned kind of economic determinism.

Defenders of this way of thinking might say, of course, that politics, ideas, and military power are important and can influence history, but that it is reasonable to assume that over the long term, economic arrangements will play a dominant role because our survival as a species depends on the economic arrangements that provide us with food and shelter and other necessities. The claim is that because we have to eat to survive, the economic arrangements that provide us with our meals will always have a special level of causal importance.

We know, however, that even people's view of what is appropriate or inappropriate to eat is shaped by culture and religious beliefs. Hunger alone is sometime not sufficient to get a person to eat food that is considered inappropriate in his or her particular culture. So even at the basic level of nutrition, we do not simply grab the optimal caloric intake. On the contrary, we pick and choose in accordance with culture, beliefs, and tastes. But if our beliefs intervene when it comes to basic biological needs, surely they also play an important role when it comes to social arrangements at a further distance from immediate survival.[2]

THE ORGANIZATION OF PRODUCTION

The first reason to be skeptical of seeing capitalism as unchanging is that it is rooted in discredited ways of thinking, such as essentialism and economic determinism. A second reason is that this way of thinking attributes causal power to the distinctly capitalist organization of production, in which employers own the means of production and attempt to make profits in a competitive market. But when we look more closely at the organization of production, we find that it does a fairly poor job in predicting how work is organized in different profit-oriented enterprises. If this approach cannot even generate accurate predictions about workplaces, how could it possibly explain the path of development of an entire society?

Remember that for those who embrace the concept of capitalism, it is not a problem that most work two hundred years ago was agricultural while most people today work in one or another kind of service occupation. They insist that the concept of capitalism remains a critical analytic tool because despite the differences, people are still working to produce things for sale on competitive markets. The claim is that farmworkers in the nineteenth century or employees of large corporations today are all under constant pressure to increase their work output in order to keep up with their most productive competitors. It is this ever-present pressure to squeeze out more output that is supposed to give the production process in capitalist societies its distinctive quality.

This argument also goes back to Karl Marx, who viewed the employment relation within capitalism as inherently antagonistic. The employer is under competitive pressure to increase profits, which means maximizing the portion of working time during which the employee's labor is producing potential profits. Exploitation is inherent in this process because workers are always paid less than the value of what they actually produce. While mainstream economists reject the Marxist idea of exploitation, they generally end up with a comparably conflictual view of the workplace.

For mainstream economics, production brings together labor, capital, and raw materials to produce outputs. The price of each of these inputs is determined on competitive markets, so the market-determined wage is appropriate compensation for labor's input. But the supervision of the process of combining inputs is in the hands of an entrepreneur who is uniquely sensitive to the signals being sent by these various markets. As he or she seeks to maximize profits, decisions must be made about how to deploy the labor force and what types of capital equipment to use. While there is no guarantee that the entrepreneur will make the correct decisions, he or she must have the authority to implement a profit-maximizing strategy. Hence, it is important that the workforce recognize and accept the authority of that entrepreneur.

Using this framework, free market economists such as Milton Friedman insist that trade unions are completely unnecessary and economically counterproductive.[3] Unions are likely to bid wages up too high and to challenge the legitimate and necessary authority of the entrepreneur. These interferences with market signals mean that resources will be used less optimally and the economy will be less productive than it would be without unions.

To be sure, many economists reject this simplistic anti-union argument. They emphasize that the actual market for labor does not work as smoothly as Friedman maintains. In reality, it is difficult for both employers and employees to create a good match between a vacant job and an individual with the capacities to fill that job well, and it is also hard for the employer to figure out the optimal structure of wages, benefits, and promotion rules for attracting the best labor force. Given these inherent imperfections in the labor market, unions can play a productive role both in the matching process and in compensation and promotion rules.[4] But most of those who make these pro-union arguments still endorse the basic ground rule of U.S. labor relations that management should not be compelled to bargain over basic business decisions such as whether to close down a particular factory or stop producing a particular product.

The central idea here is that in order to maximize profits, management must wield ultimate authority over its workforce. A well-functioning capitalist system requires that even unionized workers bend to the will of the employer. If there are going to be layoffs or reorganization of the production process or the introduction of new technologies or whatever profit maximizing requires, then management has to be able to carry out those changes.

But this is too simple, because this conflictual face of the employment relation coexists with an equally important cooperative face.[5] When managers hire workers for jobs other than the lowest-status and worst-paid positions, they are usually looking for employees with problem-solving skills who are able to take initiative. This is critical because very often top managers simply do not know how to get the optimal results out of their own systems of production. The exercise of intelligence and judgment by employees is almost always critical for increasing the firm's output and its rate of profit. But employees are unlikely to mobilize their capacities on behalf of the firm if all they see is the conflictual side of the employment relationship, where they are treated as expendable and easily replaced. So in many workplaces, there is a visible cooperative face where employees are told that they are indispensable members of a team whose coordinated efforts are vital for the success of the firm.

Workplaces differ enormously in the way that coercion and cooperation are combined. Often, it is the least skilled and most easily replaced employees who are managed by conflictual strategies that emphasize punishment and threats of being fired. Yet even in some of these cases, it is risky for management to rely only on coercion. Employees might have access to expensive equipment that could easily be sabotaged, and there might be unanticipated situations where the employer needs the worker to make a smart choice. So even in many of the settings where coercion is high, there is still some element of cooperation.

At the opposite end of the continuum, highly skilled employees are paid to be creative, and a firm has to work hard to persuade them to mobilize all of their talents and energies on a given task. Engendering this kind of cooperation usually involves telling these individuals that their input is highly valued and providing them with compensation in which they share in the gains of the firm, such as stock options or stock grants.[6] But even in highly cooperative settings, coercion does not disappear completely. Employees still have to follow certain rules, and violations can result in the employee being escorted out of the building by a security guard.

These different management strategies often give rise to a system of stratification within firms where employees closer to the bottom face more coercion and those at higher levels face much less. But sometimes firms in the same industry in the same country use dramatically different mixes of coercion and cooperation even with their average employees. One frequently discussed case in the U.S. is the comparison of the rival big box retailers Walmart and Costco. The former has been the poster child for low wages and harsh managerial strategies, while the latter pays substantially higher wages and prides itself on fostering a highly cooperative workplace.

But here is the complexity: these polar opposite management strategies have coexisted throughout the history of market societies. Saying that a firm or a society is capitalist does not tell you the relative weight of coercion and cooperation in managing its labor force. In fact, the major theorists of market societies have been debating the appropriate weight to be given to coercion and cooperation across the centuries. Adam Smith, the revered father of the idea of the "free market," was actually a proponent of the cooperative strategy. His *Wealth of Nations* frequently comments on the virtues of high wages:

> The wages of labour are the encouragement of industry which, like every other human quality, improves in proportion to the encouragement it receives. A plentiful subsistence increases the bodily strength of the labourer, and the comfortable hope of bettering his condition, and of ending his days perhaps in ease and plenty, animates him to exert that strength to the utmost. Where wages are high, accordingly, we shall always find the workmen more active, diligent, and expeditious, than where they are low.[7]

At the time that Smith wrote, most English laborers were farmworkers, and those who were kept in permanent employment were, in fact, more productive when they had a wider range of different skills. So in fact there was a correlation that Smith recognized among higher wages, higher skill levels, and more productive farms. For this reason, Smith shared the view of his mercantilist predecessors that a large and prosperous population was the goal of economic policy.

But Smith was also aware of the strategy of coercion, since artisanal work was being reorganized into a sequence of repetitive and deskilled tasks in early factories. His famous description of the pin factory recognized the enormous advances in productivity that this kind of mechanization allowed. However, Smith went on to denounce the pressure of coercive piecework because of its destructive consequences for employee health, sounding more like Karl Marx than the theorist of free markets. He ends by arguing against coercive strategies that speed up the pace of work: "It will be found, I believe, in every sort of trade, that the man who works so moderately, as to be able to work continuously, not only preserves his health the longest, but, in the course of the year, executes the greatest quantity of work."[8]

But the classical economists who followed Smith, especially Malthus and Ricardo, actually believed that there was no alternative to coercing workers; they insisted on the importance of keeping wage rates as low as possible. Malthus feared that high wages would encourage rapid and unsustainable population growth. Ricardo enunciated the iron law of wages, which required that working people be kept as close to subsistence levels as possible. It was because of their pessimistic view of wage rates that these men were labeled as practitioners of the "dismal science."

This argument between cooperative and coercive management strategies has continued unabated and unresolved through more than two hundred years. The persistence of this dispute tells us that the ongoing pressure of producing for profit on competitive markets does not tell employers how they should try to maximize output. In short, the DNA of capitalism does not even predict where a particular society falls on this continuum between cooperation and coercion in its employment system.

Apparently, that determination depends upon the specifics of a nation's political and economic history.

CONTRASTING MODELS

These explanatory difficulties become even more obvious if we begin to look in more detail at two nations that purportedly share the same capitalist DNA—the United States and Germany. While they have the same property arrangements and the same centrality of profit-making firms, there are big differences in the way they organize work and in the well-being of working people. Moreover, looking at the U.S. through the lens of Germany suggests that the policy ideas that dominated U.S. debates from the late 1970s onward have been deeply mistaken. Central to those debates is the idea that if the U.S. is to remain competitive in the global economy, it has no choice but to move to more conflictual labor relations and make significant cuts in government programs intended to benefit working people. Germany, in contrast, in its manufacturing sector, has maintained a system of cooperative employment relations, while also supporting much more generous public benefits than the U.S. And yet it has been Germany that has dominated global markets in manufacturing and the U.S. that has continued to decline as a manufacturing power.

Starting in the 1970s, business conservatives began a systematic campaign to shift the U.S. economy from a more cooperative pattern of work organization to a more coercive one. Major corporations that had in earlier decades worked out relatively cooperative arrangements with trade unions shifted toward much more conflictual strategies that involved moving work offshore, and breaking unions or forcing them to make big concessions. And, of course, almost all of the new firms that have emerged over these last forty years have been fiercely resistant to unionization. It is not a coincidence that this decades-long battle against employee rights coincided with the newfound recognition that we live in a capitalist order.

As business leaders in the 1970s took a "right turn" and aligned themselves with conservatism and free market economists, they very deliberately deployed the concept of capitalism to focus people's attention solely on the conflictual face of workplace relations.[9] They self-consciously sought to obliterate any memory of the more cooperative face of the employment relation as a way to justify moving production jobs offshore, squeezing employee wages and benefits, demonizing public-sector workers, and redefining public-sector programs such as Social Security, Medicare, and Medicaid as out-of-control entitlements that had to be slashed to avoid national bankruptcy.

Business leaders and their conservative allies insisted at every step that they were not doing these things because they were mean and greedy but because this was what was required by the free market, or capitalist economy. They were simply following the logic of a system. As Margaret Thatcher famously decreed: "There is no alternative." And it was this insistence that they were obeying the commands of the economy that made this extended campaign so effective. The reality, however, was that these claims were fictional; there was not any kind of system imperative that required a turn toward conflictual employment relations or the slashing of public programs. On the contrary, there is every reason to believe that the economy would have been stronger and more productive had the U.S. pursued more cooperative employment relationships.[10]

Moreover, the right turn of the 1970s represented a radical break with the pattern that had made the United States the world's most efficient and productive economy. The United States was the global pioneer in investing in education to create a workforce with ever-rising capacities. It was the U.S. that created the world's first system of public education, and it pioneered in making a high school education available to everyone. In fact, the level of educational attainment by the average U.S. citizen was higher than that in almost any other nation in the world until the 1980s.[11]

This was a pattern that started very early. Literacy levels were high in the early Republic, and Tocqueville observed in the 1830s that many workmen took advantage of local institutions that provided various forms of technical training to learn new skills. In the decades after the Civil War, the United States developed the most productive agricultural sector in the world. It did this by investing in agricultural research and in a system of agricultural extension that instructed farmers how they could maximize their yields per acre by choosing the right crops, the correct fertilizer, the proper amount of irrigation, and the best strategies for controlling pests and handling the uncertainties of weather. As agricultural productivity rose dramatically, the country needed fewer and fewer farmers. In 1840, people in agriculture, free and unfree, still represented 63 percent of the labor force; by 1910, the farm share of the labor force had dropped to 30.7 percent, and after that the decline only accelerated. By 2004, farmers and farm laborers represented only 1.5 percent of the labor force.[12]

As advances in agricultural technology were freeing people from the necessity of tedious and physically demanding work in farming, the country could afford to invest in higher levels of education for the population. In the first decades of the twentieth century, the "high school movement" dramatically expanded the availability of public secondary education. The same pattern continued as technological advances started to shrink the share of the population that worked in factories. As early as the 1920s, electrification and related technologies made it possible to produce an ever-larger flow of goods without increasing total hours of manufacturing labor.[13] As late as 1950, more than a quarter of the U.S. labor force had to work in manufacturing to produce the cars and dishwashers that we consume. By 2010, that figure had fallen to 10 percent even though domestically produced manufacturing output was many times higher than it had been in 1950. Across this period, society again responded by expanding the resources invested in educating the labor force. With the GI Bill, passed at the end of World War II, the U.S. dramatically increased the share of the population going to college. The more highly educated population gave the U.S. a huge competitive advantage in manufacturing and in science and innovation.

However, since the 1970s, as a result of corporate leaders' right turn, the country has reduced its investments in the labor force. With manufacturing employment falling precipitously, we should have been adjusting in the same way that we did in response to declining agricultural employment, by increasing our collective investments in education. Instead, our level of spending on education stagnated. The main reason was the ongoing tax revolt, which placed fiscal pressures on all levels of government. The federal government eliminated revenue-sharing flows that had earlier gone to the states, and both state and local governments faced a mismatch between growing obligations and ongoing pressures to avoid tax increases. The result has been stagnant levels of public school spending. Moreover, as the share of children in the U.S. growing up in poverty has continued to rise, the school system has been unable to do anything about dropout rates in minority communities, which remain shockingly high. The consequence has been that international comparisons of adult literacy now show the U.S. lagging well behind other nations.

One of the most important shifts has been the sharp decline in support for public higher education by state governments.[14] These governments have pushed the cost of college on to students and their families. For many young people from poor and working-class families, the strategy of pursuing mobility through advanced education simply became too risky to try. Even in the middle class, it has become common for students to graduate from college with levels of debt between $100,000 and $150,000— the kind of amounts that people used to take out in home mortgages.[15]

The end of the long-established pattern in which the U.S. invested to produce the best-educated labor force in the world has had real consequences. The U.S. is now being beaten in international economic competition by nations that have been willing to increase their educational investments. One can see this most clearly in the comparison between the United States and Germany, which has remained a leading manufacturing nation by investing in skills and by creating institutions that strengthen the cooperative face of employment relations.

GERMANY'S MANUFACTURING ADVANTAGE

The right turn that U.S. businesses took in the 1970s was legitimated by the claim that a capitalist system requires conflictual employment relations and cutbacks in public spending. This argument attributes U.S. economic difficulties to the misguided legacy of Franklin Roosevelt's New Deal, which interfered with the economy's underlying dynamism. The right turn resulted in a decline of trade unions in the U.S., the movement of significant parts of U.S. manufacturing to low-wage sites abroad, and diminishing investments in educating the country's labor force. In the meantime, other countries have followed a different model. They have been increasing their educational investments and in the German case, sustaining the cooperative face of work relations in manufacturing. As a consequence, Germany has become the global leader in high-end manufacturing.[16]

The reality is that those U.S. business leaders and their conservative economic allies failed to understand the links between a better-educated population and a more dynamic economy. The links work through three distinct channels. First, better-educated workers can master the complex technologies of high-quality production of goods and services better than less-educated populations. Second, a better-educated labor force is likelier to make the breakthroughs needed for innovative new products and processes.[17] Finally, nations increasingly prosper in the global marketplace by having more sophisticated consumers who know how to consume cutting-edge new technologies like the internet, cellular phones, and new generations of more energy-efficient vehicles.[18] The nations with the best-educated people and the highest measured rates of literacy are also the places with the most productive economies and the highest standards of living.

But the claim that upgrading the labor force is the key to prosperity requires some qualification. There is the harsh reality that millions of manufacturing jobs have left the richer countries to take advantage of cheap labor overseas. This pattern is certainly not unique to the U.S. Germany, Japan, and most other developed nations now import many manufactured goods from overseas. The process started with garments, shoes, and toys in the

1950s, and then progressed to consumer electronics and then to increasingly sophisticated products. Today, pretty much everything for sale in big box retailers like Walmart and Best Buy has a "made in China" label. This trend is not just limited to manufacturing; increasingly, service labor such as editing, writing software, and producing architectural drawings is being done overseas in India or the Philippines by employees who are paid a fraction of what comparable employees make in the United States. There is now even medical and dental tourism for U.S. citizens who travel abroad to have procedures done so cheaply that they come out ahead even after factoring in travel costs.

For more than a generation, this threat of employers taking advantage of cheap labor from abroad has been used to persuade people in the U.S. that they have to accept lower wages, fewer benefits, and harsher working conditions. For every workplace that has literally shut down and moved abroad, there are two or three more where the threat of such action has enabled employers to force employees to accept work conditions they would otherwise reject. The dramatic decline in the percentage of employees in the U.S. who are represented by unions is closely linked to cheap foreign labor. Employers in unionized industries moved many jobs overseas, and the continuing threat of shifting production overseas has helped doom many union-organizing campaigns.[19]

And the public has been repeatedly told that there is nothing that can be done about this because it has long been proven that something called "free trade"—where firms are free to locate production in the area of the world where it is most profitable to produce—is absolutely essential for prosperity. In fact, this specific notion of free trade has been integrated into the definition of capitalism; it is a global system that imposes few restraints on the ability of businesses to locate where their profits will be greatest.

However, the falseness of these business claims becomes clear when we look at the experience over the last generation of Germany. In contrast to the United States, Germany has continued to be a major exporter of manufactured goods, with about 27 percent of its labor force still in the manufacturing sector.[20] Moreover, German manufacturing workers continue to enjoy wages, benefits, and working conditions that are far better than comparable workers in the United States.[21] How is this possible? Should not the logic of global free trade have done the same thing to Germany's manufacturing sector as happened to the U.S.?

Part of the explanation is that German manufacturing firms have had a better sense of the cooperative face of the employment relationship. For sophisticated manufactured goods such as automobiles, appliances, and machine tools, wages for manufacturing workers represent only 5 to 10 percent of the product's total costs. So once one calculates the transportation costs and various hidden costs of moving production to China or some other low-wage country, it often does not make economic sense for firms to seek out the cheapest labor.

One of these hidden costs is quality control. The more complex the product, the more difficult it is to maintain quality; the problem becomes severe when the production process is occurring thousands of miles away from corporate headquarters. So it is not uncommon for firms that move production abroad to lose market share because of diminished quality. Another hidden cost is the possible loss of control over the firm's intellectual property. Firms operating in China sometimes find new firms sprouting up to compete with pirated versions of their own products.

Perhaps the most important hidden cost occurs when thousands of miles separate a company's research and development operations from its production facilities. With technologically complex products, ramping up to mass production is the last and often most critical step of research and development. With flat-panel display screens or advanced batteries, figuring out how to mass-produce the product is one of the biggest technological challenges, so the firm needs some of its best engineers working on the shop floor with production workers. Moreover, this is not just a one-time challenge; such products are likely to be repeatedly upgraded and modified, so there will be continuous changes to the techniques of mass production. We now have ample evidence that most of the firms that remain at the technological cutting edge are now keeping research and development and production in close proximity.[22]

This co-location has been one of the great advantages of German manufacturing firms. Even when they shift some production to cheaper labor locations, they are careful to keep the more sophisticated production processes close to their research facilities. These choices have been facilitated by German public policies. Germany has set up mechanisms that give unionized manufacturing employees considerable influence over corporate decision making. Codetermination means that employee representatives sit on the top-level corporate boards, and factories have works councils that are a formal mechanism through which unionized workers and management come up with shared solutions to ongoing problems.

The consequence is that in the automobile industry, for example, German workers have been able to negotiate the specific terms on which their firms move some of their production to lower-wage countries in Eastern Europe. German workers have agreed to let firms move production of cheaper models to these new factories on the condition that firms create new, higher-quality jobs at German factories. Domestic employment within the German auto industry has continued to rise even as the firms build more plants abroad. Moreover, Germany continues to produce the high-end Mercedes, BMWs, and Porsches in German factories that retain their global reputation for quality and continued technical advances.[23] Similar patterns exist in other industries. For example, Germany continues to dominate global markets for high-end machine tools, most of which are produced by middle-sized German factories where workers are highly skilled and well compensated.

Finally, through collaboration between firms, unions, and the government, Germany has built up an effective system for providing employees with the skills required for advanced manufacturing. A good part of this occurs through an apprenticeship program that continues to attract applicants of high quality.[24] The U.S. has nothing comparable. The very weak system of training programs financed by the federal government tends to focus on preparing individuals from marginalized populations for low-wage employment. The apprenticeship route for teaching skilled trades has largely died out. Those communities that have tried to attract or retain manufacturing employers have been forced to improvise training programs relying on local community colleges. Hence U.S. employers often argue that if they are going to have to train workers at their own expense, they might as well train more compliant and cheaper workers overseas.

In sum, a lot of the offshoring of manufacturing that happened in the U.S. was not inevitable. The U.S. could have retained more manufacturing capacity if it had had better public policies and if there had not been such a strong management fashion in favor of outsourcing. The same is true for some of the skilled service jobs that are now also moving offshore. The reality is that bad public policies intersected with intense managerial enthusiasm for cutting labor costs. Because of the intense pressures on firms to maximize shareholder value that began in the 1980s, shifting production overseas became a dogma for U.S. corporate managers. For a generation, managers and MBA students in the U.S. were instructed that it was always better to move production to China or other overseas sites. In short, it was irrational choices made by corporate managers and public officials that led to the precipitous decline of U.S. manufacturing.

THE REALITY OF TRANSFORMATION

There is still another reason to be wary of the view of capitalism as a fixed and unchanging system. Even in nations such as Germany and China, which have become major exporters of manufactured goods, the percentage of the labor force that works in manufacturing has been declining for decades now. The decline has been even sharper in the United States. And, when one looks at the data more closely, the decline of classical production jobs such as working on assembly lines has been even more dramatic. Many of the people still recorded as working in manufacturing are doing clerical jobs or are repairing machinery. Moreover, these trends are bound to accelerate everywhere as sophisticated machine tools and robots become ever cheaper.[25]

This is where the habitation society argument made in chapter 2 is relevant. In a habitation society, many repetitive jobs will be automated out of existence. Toll collectors on highways and ticket sellers on transit systems are being rapidly displaced by computer technologies. As these trends continue, most of the remaining jobs will involve human judgment, skills in dealing with other human beings, and quite often, a degree of creativity and problem-solving skills. For that reason, the shift to a habitation society favors a broader shift toward more cooperative employment relations.

To be sure, such a shift is so far hard to envision in the United States, where employers have held firmly to the idea of conflictual and coercive work organization. But the logic of a more benign form of work organization becomes very clear when one thinks about hospitals and facilities that take care of the elderly. These are, not coincidentally, two of the most rapidly growing sites of employment in most developed market societies. Many of these facilities treat their employees quite badly; they impose heavy workloads and provide very low pay, especially for those who clean and do other menial tasks.

However, these conflictual practices undermine the core mission of these institutions. For example, sloppy and inadequate cleaning in such facilities can lead to the spread of microorganisms that bring infection and death for both patients and staff. The logic of upgrading the cleaning staff and training them to be on the lookout for potential biohazards is extremely strong. Similarly, the frontline employees who feed and bathe the elderly can have a major impact on residents' quality of life.[26] In short, conflictual employment relations make very little sense in these types of workplaces.

But then the issue of fairness enters the picture. In agricultural society and in industrial society, it was easy to see the logic of organizing society into distinct classes with radically different standards of living. If some people did not work in the fields all day or toil on an assembly line for forty or fifty hours a week, other people would not be able to eat or purchase an automobile. One can question the justice of an arrangement where those who work the hardest got the least reward, but the fundamental reality was that some people had to accept work that was backbreaking for the good of others.

Now, however, this necessity is disappearing because of our success in getting machines and computers to do routine work. In developed societies like the United States, the number of people who have to do hard physical labor to provide us with fruits, vegetables, machinery, and new buildings is now so small that we can afford to pay them a decent wage and organize the work to make it less burdensome and less alienating. At the same time, we can also afford to make the work that others do in universities, hospitals, elder-care facilities, and government agencies more satisfying and humane. This is the point of substituting machines, including increasingly intelligent machines, for human labor; it makes it possible to reorganize work to make it more compelling and more satisfying for human beings.

CONFRONTING CLASS POWER

Up until now, I have ignored the most compelling argument about how capitalist property arrangements structure an entire social order. This is the idea that private ownership of the means of production generates a fundamental divide between a small group that owns most of society's productive capacity and everybody else. And it is the ongoing efforts of members of this owning class—we can call them the 1 percent—to preserve and enhance their position that determines what can and cannot occur in this kind of class-divided society. In short, capitalist property relations give the owning class extraordinary power that it uses to influence politics and every other aspect of the society's development.

This is an important point, and in earlier chapters I stressed that our society has already taken a dangerous turn from democracy to oligarchy as the 1 percent have become even more powerful. But I also want to insist that how much class power is exerted by an ownership class is not a constant; it is a variable. It ebbs and flows depending on a number of factors, including the organization and mobilization of those in society who are trying to challenge that power.

Well before there was capitalism, there were owners who appropriated the largest share of society's wealth and exerted disproportionate influence over entire societies. This is not something new and distinctive about economies organized around private profit; it occurred in ancient empires, in Rome and Greece, and in feudal Europe. The distinctive feature of market economies, as argued earlier, is that they have flourished in democratic societies, and democratic institutions place some constraints and limits on the class power of those who own society's wealth.

The nature of those constraints and limits fluctuates significantly over time. So, for example, Thomas Piketty's data show that there are big shifts that occur over time in the share of income and wealth that are controlled by the top 1 percent of households in England, France, and the United States. In France, for example, Piketty estimates that the top 1 percent owned 60 percent of all the wealth in 1910, but that fell to almost 20 percent in 1970 and was still below 25 percent in 2010. In the U.S., the change was less dramatic—from 45 percent in 1910 to a low of 29 percent in 1970 and back to 32 percent in 2010.[27] One of the main factors influencing these shifts over time are tax policies, which determine what share of its income the top 1 percent is able to keep. In the U.S., for example, in the 1950s, the top marginal income tax rate was 91 percent, but is now 39.6 percent.[28]

If class power were a constant, one would expect the top 1 percent share of wealth to remain at an extremely high level. But the fact that both tax rates and wealth holding fluctuate over time suggests that the exercise of class power is not a simple matter. Its efficacy can and does vary significantly. For example, Piketty stresses that the period of the First World War and of postwar reconstruction witnessed a dramatic fall in the share of income going to the top 1 percent. In that war, each nation had to mobilize the children of the working class to kill on an industrial scale, so it was a political necessity to make economic concessions to working-class voters. At the same time, during periods of warfare and postwar reconstruction, the government has much more control over the economy; the rich cannot threaten to withhold investments simply because profits are not high enough.[29] Moreover, the period after World War I saw the biggest strike wave ever recorded; working-class militancy forced governments to make concessions.

But other factors also shape the exercise of class power. Sometimes, it is just ten or twenty families that own most of a nation's productive resources, but in other cases, as with the U.S. today, ownership might be spread out across a million households. The smaller the owning class, the easier it is for them to coordinate their efforts and exert pressure in the same direction. Moreover, whether an owning class is large or small, it must struggle with internal differences. Those who make their money through extracting minerals from the earth might have differences with those who own factories or those who own banks. Sometimes, it might be easy to bridge these differences, but at other times, it can be extremely difficult. And when the owning class becomes seriously divided, it is far more vulnerable to outside pressures.

So private ownership of society's wealth does create a reality of class power because the owners have far more resources than ordinary citizens and they have strategic leverage over society's productive assets. But these owners are far from omnipotent, and their class power has been challenged for centuries. In fact, pretty much every major reform from equality before the law to universal suffrage to the progressive income tax to trade union rights was won against the opposition of most of the owning class. There is no way of knowing in advance what other reforms could be won if this class power were effectively challenged.

This is precisely why I am attacking the idea that there is something similar to a genetic code that determines what a society with private pursuit of profits will look like. That way of thinking simply bolsters the class power of wealth holders because it leads to the assumption that the future will look very similar to the present. The reality is that thirty years from now, the U.S. might still have a private ownership economy, but the society could look completely different from the present in the extent of poverty, in the degree of income and wealth inequality, and in the power exercised by the 1 percent.

In other words, our future will not be determined by the logic of an economic system, but by the outcome of the political struggles to challenge the power and authority of the owning class. We simply do not know in advance if there are limits to the reforms that can be won that would improve the quality of life for people in the bottom half of the income distribution or that would move us closer to the democratic ideal where every citizen has an equal chance to shape our laws and government policies. The reality is that there have simply been too many transformations and too many discontinuities in the development of market societies for anybody to assert with authority that such reform struggles are exercises in futility.

CONCLUSION

The conventional view is that capitalism is a system with an unchanging core created by the fact that profit-making firms must struggle for survival in competitive markets. Many analysts imagine that capitalism has a fixed DNA that determines the structure of the entire society. But this way of thinking depends on seeing one essential feature of a social order as determining everything else. It also rests on the assumption that the economy is always the most important determinant of social processes; political power, military force, and ideology must be relegated to secondary importance.

This approach also leads to an overemphasis on the conflictual nature of work relations resulting from the pressure on employers to minimize wages and benefits while simultaneously maximizing worker output. It is this understanding of work relations that has been at the core of the campaign by business leaders in the U.S. since the early 1970s to lower wages and benefits and cut back government entitlement spending. But the workplace also has a cooperative face, and there are many examples where collaborative arrangements between employees and their managers are effective at sustaining profitability. Moreover, with technologically sophisticated manufacturing and the growing importance of innovation, there is mounting evidence that cooperative workplace strategies are the best way to make firms profitable.

In sum, the debates over both workplaces and entitlements in the U.S. have been systematically distorted by a failure to recognize that nations that invest in their workforces are actually more effective in international trade competition. Those who see only the conflictual face of employment relations simply cannot make sense out of the continuing success of Germany and the Scandinavian nations in the global market. Here again, the prevailing concept of capitalism does not illuminate reality; it obscures it.

Finally, there is the argument that the unified nature of capitalist societies results from the class power exerted by the owning class. But the fact that the wealth share of the French top 1 percent dropped from 60 percent in 1910 to 20 percent in 1970 suggests that class power is a variable and has been effectively challenged in certain historical periods. To be sure, over the past forty years, the wealth share of the top 1 percent has risen sharply in the United States and the United Kingdom, suggesting a strengthening of class power. But this hardly suggests that this power is unassailable. In fact, if fewer people believed that extreme inequality of income and wealth is an inevitable part of a capitalism system, it would be easier to mobilize social movements to challenge the class power of the wealthy.

CHAPTER SIX

The Illusion of Global Order Organized by Capitalism

The world we live in is obviously a very dangerous place. At least nine nations have nuclear weapons and even a handful of these being detonated could make significant portions of the planet uninhabitable. Terrorist groups have been active across many countries, unleashing sudden and indiscriminate violent attacks. Skirmishes and hot spots in various parts of the world, including the Middle East, the Ukraine, the Korean peninsula, and the South China Sea, could easily escalate into a larger war. We also face the threat of catastrophic climate change, which causes extreme weather events such as droughts, floods, and superstorms that put millions of people at risk. And there continues to be the threat of new epidemics that could kill as large a share of the world's population as died in the bubonic plague in the Middle Ages.

One of the ways that people have coped with the anxieties of living in such a dangerous world is to imagine that the sources of chaos and disorder are ancient and archaic, and that they are gradually being displaced by a new and rational social order that can stabilize the planet, reduce the threat of war, and encourage global cooperation to solve shared problems. This idea was expressed by Thomas Friedman in his formulation that no two nations that had McDonald's franchises had ever waged war against each other.[1] He meant that the spread of market institutions was bringing order, predictability, and rationality, which would ultimately defeat the forces of chaos.[2]

Underlying this line of argument is the belief that if we could turn the whole world into one unified marketplace, there would no longer be a need for war. Nations would continue to compete and jockey for advantage, but they would do it by developing new technologies and new products that make their citizens wealthier. And since technological progress in one nation is likely to spill over to other nations, this benign competition will end up making everybody better off. In place of the zero sum conflicts of warfare, there would be the positive sum competition of the marketplace.

But in much the same way that free market theorists pretend that there is very little need for government to manage the economy at the national level, this view requires believing that agreement on the rules governing global economic competition can and will occur easily and naturally. Everyone is supposed to recognize that global capitalism requires free trade and the free movement of capital and give the same interpretation to those abstract concepts. But the reality is that markets cannot organize society by themselves nationally and they cannot do so globally.

The historical reality is one of fierce conflicts and disagreements over the rules governing the global marketplace, since any particular set of rules will benefit some nations, some firms, and some individuals and hurt others. Moreover, when there has been some orderly arrangement governing the global economy, it has been the result not of some imaginary and spontaneous global consensus, but because a particular nation—first England and then the United States—exercised global hegemony and used its economic, political, and military superiority to impose order on other nations.

The specific rules governing international economic transactions, furthermore, can be hugely consequential because they shape the balance of economic and political power between social groups within nations. The gold standard in the nineteenth century, for example, bolstered the political and economic power of economic elites and made it much more difficult for working people to win important political and economic reforms. And it continues to be the case that the exercise of class power by dominant economic groups is often facilitated by a specific set of global economic rules.

This particular part of the capitalist illusion has three separate elements. First, people fail to pay attention to the global institutions and rules because they have been persuaded that global capitalism is self-organizing; they imagine that a global capitalist order sprang up spontaneously. Second, they do not understand the importance of the specific institutions and rules that exist at the global level. They do not see that these have a huge impact on political struggles within nations. Finally, they fail to recognize that the global order can be restructured and reformed to be consistent with such political goals as environmental sustainability and greater equality of income and wealth.

THE PROBLEM OF CAPITAL FLIGHT

To dispel this particular illusion, it is useful to begin with a concrete example of the linkage between global economic rules and domestic political conflicts. At various times, the organization of the global economy has made it easy for the wealthy to move capital across national boundaries. This capacity facilitates the use of capital flight as a political weapon against democratically elected governments.

The scenario begins when a newly elected government comes to power with the promise to raise taxes on the rich and strengthen the bargaining power of poorly paid workers. Members of the owning class are likely to mobilize against this threat by using standard tactics such as lobbying, protests, and lawsuits. But if such measures prove to be ineffective in stopping the new government's plans, some wealth holders are likely to shift some of their capital overseas.[3] They might, for example, close domestic bank accounts and move the proceeds to a Swiss bank. They can justify this by saying that the government's policies will fuel inflation, which will, in turn, lower the value of the national currency, so shifting assets abroad is simply a form of self-protection.

But as the amount of fleeing capital increases, it often poses a fundamental challenge to the government. Large outflows of capital usually lower the value of the nation's currency, with the immediate consequence that imported goods become more expensive, so that many citizens will no longer be able to afford things they earlier were able to purchase. Governments are usually forced to respond to these increased capital outflows by imposing austerity measures that slash government outlays and increase unemployment. Such policies tend to reduce political support for the government and quite often will force the embattled administration to abandon its earlier reform ideas. In short, capital flight has been an extremely important part of the arsenal of class power.

However, there have been times when the weapon of capital flight was not readily available because of international agreements. For example, from the start of World War II until the late 1970s, most developed nations placed limits on the ability of individuals and firms to move capital abroad. While these capital controls started in reaction to the outbreak of World War II, they were incorporated into the postwar Bretton Woods international monetary order. They continued because they made it much easier for nations to manage their international accounts.[4] While some capital flight could still occur even with the controls, the reality is that this political weapon was effectively blunted. As a consequence, the class power of wealth holders was weakened, and they had to acquiesce in reforms they did not like. It is no coincidence that this same period of time saw lower levels of concentrated wealth and income inequality and significant expansion of public provision.[5]

But capital flight is only one example of the links between global processes and national politics. Just in the last few years, we saw a left-wing government come to power in Greece with a promise to the voters that it would renegotiate the painful austerity that had been imposed on that country by the European Community and the International Monetary Fund. But sure enough, these same parties made continued financial support for Greece contingent on the government abandoning its campaign promises, and the new government was forced to submit.

The point is that the rules governing international economic transactions are extremely important; they make a huge difference in the outcome of battles over economic and social policy within nations. But these rules have changed repeatedly over the last two hundred years because they are closely linked to the complex politics of global hegemony. In the nineteenth century and up through World War I, England as the global hegemon shaped the international rules governing economic transactions. In the mid-twentieth century, the role of hegemon shifted to the United States, and since then the U.S. has exerted disproportionate influence over the governance of global economic transactions. But global hegemony is not a constant; the power of the hegemon relative to other nations tends to vary over time, and those shifts have implications.

However, most discussions of the logic of capitalism or the needs of the capitalist system ignore the centrality of these international rules because of the fantasy that global capitalism is self-organizing.[6] This makes it difficult to see the global rules as a critical terrain of contestation despite the fact that social movements have been successful in forcing changes in global rules and global institutions.

THE ROOTS OF THE PROBLEM

Failing to understand the variability and the importance of the specific rules governing international economic transactions is a problem that goes back to Karl Marx. In his efforts to make sense of the newly emergent economic system in Europe in the middle of the nineteenth century, Marx made an understandable analytic error that has caused confusion ever since. Marx observed two distinct phenomena. First, there was the rapid growth across Western European countries and North America of profit-oriented firms that were hiring workers to produce goods on competitive markets. Second, England, the first country to industrialize, was using its economic and military power to get other nations to accept its proposed ground rules for organizing the global economy. England pushed other countries to embrace freedom of navigation on the high seas, to abolish trade barriers, and to adopt the international gold standard.

Marx jumped to the erroneous conclusion that these two different phenomena were simply two sides of the same coin. It seemed logical that as England had been the first nation to embrace industrial capitalism, it was leading the way to create the global arrangements that capitalism required. To be sure, Marx had no illusions that England was acting benevolently. He recognized that England's foreign policy was designed to make that nation's capitalists even richer. But he also imagined that the arrangements and rules that England was imposing on the world were exactly what a global system of capitalism required. In his mind, there was no real choice around free trade and the gold standard; they were the arrangements that best fit with a global system of capitalism.

So Marx treated England's great power politics as part of the unfolding logic of global capitalism. When the English navy bombarded the port city of an independent nation to force the government to agree to dismantle barriers to England's export of goods and capital, Marx saw the English making the world safe for capitalism. In his approach, capitalism expanded globally both because profit-oriented firms took root in different societies and through a simultaneous process of coercion, led by England, to break down barriers to the spread of this new economic system across the globe.

Marx's analytic error has been replicated in contemporary accounts of how a capitalist system functions. It is common to argue that capitalism became global through the emergence of profit-oriented firms within nations that transform production and the basic institutions of society, and through leading capitalist nations imposing global rules that coax or coerce every nation on the planet to open themselves to the transformation driven by profit-oriented firms. To be sure, some nations have tried to resist those pressures, as with those that embraced state socialism in the twentieth century. By the turn of the twenty-first century, however, effective resistance had largely disappeared with the possible exceptions of Cuba and North Korea. The long series of interventions—both overt and covert—through which the U.S. has toppled unfriendly regimes in the decades since World War II are often seen as part of this process.[7]

But why should we see such foreign interventions as the expression of the inner logic of a capitalist world economy? Why not see what England did in the nineteenth century and what the U.S. has done since World War II as what great powers have done to other countries since the time of the ancient empires? Across the millennia, great powers have used their economic and military power to coerce other societies in order to extract some of their wealth. The techniques vary over time, but the goal is to get other nations to agree to transactions that transfer wealth from the weaker to the stronger.[8] This is a global dynamic that long predates capitalism.

In short, it was not the imperatives of global capitalism that shaped England's foreign policy in the nineteenth century, but rather the interests of England's ruling class. In fact, the period in which England pushed for policies of global economic liberalism was a relatively brief segment of its global hegemony. England did link the value of the pound to a fixed quantity of gold in the years immediately after the Napoleonic Wars, but it was not until the 1870s that England pushed most other nations in Europe to adopt the gold standard. In fact, the period of the classical gold standard was relatively brief, lasting from 1880 to the outbreak of World War I—a small fraction of the total time that England was the global hegemon.

England's commitment to global free trade was also relatively short and uneven.[9] England did not do away with agricultural tariffs until 1846, and laws restricting the export of textile machinery were only repealed in 1843. Moreover, England's pioneering industrialization relied heavily on the global empire that England had assembled in the eighteenth century. English merchants traded fine cotton textiles that they obtained from colonial India for fresh shipments of African slaves, who then produced vast quantities of cotton on plantations in the Caribbean and the American South. This abundant cotton was then used to fuel England's vast production of lower-quality cotton textiles. Many of those inferior English machine-made textiles were exported back to India and China, where the English used imperial power to eliminate the competition from higher-quality local cotton goods.[10]

This meant that the period in which England fully embraced free trade was also quite brief. It was already over by the 1880s, when England began expanding its eighteenth-century empire by joining the European rush to exert colonial control over Africa. As early as the 1880s, the English were debating whether to hold on to free trade or opt for a system of imperial tariffs that would wall off the empire from foreign competitors.

Parallel arguments can be made about the period in which the United States has been the global hegemon. During and immediately after World War II, the U.S. put pressure on the European powers to dismantle their colonial empires in order to bring the world closer to global free trade. Yet, as early as the Marshall Plan in 1947, the U.S. muted its anticolonialism, recognizing that European recovery depended on restoring prewar patterns in which favorable trading relations with colonies and former colonies allowed European nations to offset their trade deficits with the U.S. Moreover, the U.S. retained strongly protectionist elements in its own trade policies. The Buy America Act, originally passed in 1933, continues to give preference to domestic producers for government procurement contracts.[11] Significant barriers to foreign imports of manufactured goods were kept in place up through the 1980s, and imports of foreign agricultural commodities such as cotton and sugar are blocked to this day.

Most importantly, much of the emphasis of U.S. international trade policies since the 1980s has centered not on classical issues of tariffs but on questions of "intellectual property." Driven particularly by pharmaceutical companies, Hollywood, and the computer industry, the U.S. has exerted pressure on other nations to honor the government-granted monopolies that have been created by patent or copyright protection. This has very little to do with historic discussions of free trade, which were based on the model of widespread competition to produce products at the best possible price. For decades now, when the U.S. talks about free trade, it really refers to other nations recognizing and enforcing the corporate monopolies facilitated by the U.S. government.

Similar arguments can be made about U.S. international monetary policies. The U.S. presided over the Bretton Woods regime from 1944 to 1971; that system made the U.S. dollar the world's major currency. During this period, there was a substantial overlap between U.S. national interest and the world economy's need for a stable global international economic regime. But by the late 1960s, the U.S. was finding it increasingly difficult to meet its obligations under the Bretton Woods system. Starting with Nixon's decision to close the gold window in 1971, the U.S. chose to maximize its own freedom of action regardless of the consequences for other nations. This policy culminated in the

Reagan administration's decision in 1983 to force other nations to finance the chronic U.S. balance of payments deficit.[12]

In short, the periods in which the self-interest of England and the United States produced international economic policies that worked to create an optimal environment for global economic expansion were relatively brief. Most of the time, these great powers pursued their own interests even when those needs diverged from those of other major powers. The problem, of course, is that theorists of a global capitalist order want to pretend that this system just emerges naturally without the exercise of political power.

A DIFFERENT FRAMEWORK

To make sense of the actual evolution of the global economy, it is essential to recognize three distinct but interconnected processes—the spread of profit-oriented firms, the pursuit of self-interest by global hegemons, and the institutionalization of a global structure of rules governing economic transactions. The spread of profit-oriented firms across the globe tends to produce highly uneven economic outcomes. As argued earlier, when profit-oriented firms coexist with effective democratic institutions, the result has often been sustained improvements in living standards. However, when profit-oriented firms exist within authoritarian regimes or regimes that are only superficially democratic, the result tends to be economic stagnation. Economies based on resource extraction either through mining or plantation agriculture tend to be dominated by oligarchic elites and are profitable but not dynamic.

The second process is that of the rise and decline of great powers. This pattern repeats itself because exerting control over a wide geographical expanse undermines the economic vitality that fueled the great power's earlier rise. The military outlays required to support a hegemonic position tend to subvert prosperity at home. Moreover, investment flows tend to shift away from domestic industries and toward the empire.[13] This familiar pattern of imperial overreach long predated the rise of profit-oriented production.

The third process is distinctly modern; it began in the middle of the nineteenth century. This is the ever-increasing formalization of global rules to manage the world economy. This process became visible in the middle of the nineteenth century with international agreements around freedom of navigation and conventions to ensure the enforcement of patents and copyrights. Since the twentieth century, the process of creating such international agreements has accelerated, and formalization has been pushed further by the creation of new governance institutions to implement particular agreements, including the League of Nations, the United Nations, the Bretton Woods institutions, the World Trade Organization, and most recently, the Group of Twenty. Along with these broad-ranging global organizations, there are also many specialized organizations that set standards or seek greater global uniformity in environmental, business, and regulatory practices.[14]

These three distinct processes intersect in complex ways that create considerable variability over time. In contrast to the illusion that capitalism has been stable for several centuries, looking at these three interacting patterns gives us instead a story of turbulence and continuous change. Since great powers rise and fall, the ability of England and then the United States to make the world safe for the expansion of their business firms shifts over time. Moreover, as a dominant power struggles with the dilemma of preserving its international position even as it contends with the problem of global overreach, its global strategies are also likely to change.

These shifts have real consequences. For example, when a hegemonic power is at its height, other nations are usually respectful toward the global rules that are pushed by the hegemon. But when other nations see the great power struggling, they are more likely to find ways to work around or even directly violate the rules. In the period after 1873, for example, there was a flowering of protectionist trade policies as many developed nations used tariffs to gain greater control over their foreign economic transactions. They continued to adhere to the gold standard, but the tariffs undermined the global free trade regime that was an essential part of England's vision for the world. Similarly, since 1999, the member nations of the World Trade Organization have been unable to agree on a new round of trade liberalization measures. With U.S. hegemony declining, the developing nations have refused to make further concessions unless the richer nations agree to major shifts in agricultural policies that would open up developed markets to more imported agricultural goods.

The third process—the increased formalization of global rules and the creation of global governance institutions—has greatly benefited profit-oriented firms. Businesses that operate across national boundaries want and need rules that will lower the costs of these transactions through standardization, so they can do things the same way in multiple nations. Similarly, hegemonic powers, especially when they are at their strongest, tend to support this process of formalization since many of the business firms that benefit will be their own. However, formalization is also attractive to other great powers because they too have many businesses that want to expand internationally. Rising powers also see the formalization of rules as a possible way to restrain and limit the authority of the global hegemon. As the relative power of the global hegemon starts to decline, other nations are likely to support global institutions that could potentially discourage arbitrary actions by the hegemon.

However, the process of hegemonic decline can also work to disrupt formalized global institutions. This is what happened after World War I. The League of Nations was created as an international governance institution that exerted strong pressure for the restoration of the gold standard. However, England had been sufficiently weakened by the war that it could no longer provide the flows of credit that had helped to lubricate the global economy in the three decades before the war. The U.S. filled some of this void with foreign capital flows until 1929, but the U.S. was not ready to take on the kind of global leadership that England had exercised. As a consequence, when the global depression worsened, both the gold standard and the League of Nations collapsed.

There are some parallels now as U.S. global power is in decline and is increasingly challenged by China's rise. The International Monetary Fund has become more central to managing the global economy since the meltdown in 2008, but it took the U.S. Congress five years to approve a carefully negotiated global agreement to reallocate quotas and voting rights in the Fund. The U.S. is having greater difficulties making the global institutions that it created work effectively, and the Chinese have recently intensified their challenge by constructing their own international infrastructure bank despite open opposition from the U.S.

It is possible that as in the 1930s, much of the formal institutional structure of global governance that was built during the period of U.S. hegemony will come crashing down as the U.S.

declines. Certainly, the Trump administration did follow through on its threat to withdraw from the Paris climate accord, and its commitment to the World Trade Organization and the International Monetary Fund remains uncertain. But it is also possible that something historically unprecedented could happen. The existing structures of global governance could prove robust enough to manage the process of U.S. hegemonic decline. In this scenario, international institutions would be reconfigured to recognize China's rise and the U.S. decline without China having to take on the full set of hegemonic responsibilities. If this were to happen, it would mark an extraordinary historical turning point since the existence of a global order would for the first time be independent of the exercise of power by a single global hegemon.

By recognizing these three distinct processes—the spread of profit-oriented firms, the rise and fall of hegemonic powers, and the formalization of global institutions and rules—it is possible to develop an effective periodization of recent global economic arrangements. We can distinguish five distinct periods:

1. The classical gold standard, from 1880 to 1914.
2. The gold standard in crisis, from 1914 to 1933.
3. The interregnum, from 1933 to 1945.
4. The Bretton Woods era, from 1945 to 1973.
5. The floating rates era, from 1973 to 2018.

There are huge differences across these five periods in the degree to which global arrangements constrained and limited the political and economic choices available to developed nations. In periods 1, 2, and 5, the global arrangements made it extremely difficult to negotiate an effective class compromise between working people and employers because of strong pressures to restrain wage gains and limit government outlays. In periods 3 and 4, in contrast, there was much more space to construct such class compromises. In other words, different global arrangements work to tilt countries toward more conflictual or more cooperative employment relations.

This periodization suggests that Marx's analytic error had two very important consequences that we are still living with today. First, imagining that global financial arrangements are an automatic reflex of profit-maximizing economic relations makes it impossible to see that these global arrangements are a regime that can be altered through political action. Social movement efforts to reshape the global rules of commerce started with the campaign to end the international slave trade in England in the late eighteenth century and have continued down to the present. But it is particularly since the 1990s that global social movements have emerged to challenge the global order in ways that would foster equality, democracy, and environmental sustainability. However, these efforts still have not mobilized the broad support needed to produce changes on the scale that is required.[15]

Second, Marx's error contributed to the naturalization of these global rules, where they are seen as both unchanging and inevitable correlates of global capitalism. Karl Polanyi made this point very clearly in his account of the global debates that occurred at the end of World War I.[16] He noted the historical irony that even the Bolsheviks who had recently seized power in Russia endorsed the international consensus in favor of restoring the gold standard. In Polanyi's view, that restoration was a tragic error that led directly to the Great Depression, the rise of fascism, and World War II. Polanyi's point was that if people could have seen that the gold standard was just one among many different possible ways to organize global finance, these disastrous outcomes could have been avoided.

Naturalization means seeing these global arrangements as unchanging structures. But as the periodization suggests, there have been five different regimes over the past 135 years, with each one lasting an average of only twenty-seven years. The shortcomings of our current regime were most obviously displayed with the severity of the 2008–2009 global financial crisis. In the years since that crisis, global growth has been extremely sluggish, with the world economy in constant danger of sliding back into recession. And yet no serious global debate has emerged about creating a new and better set of global arrangements. This testifies again to Polanyi's point; humanity pays a huge price for naturalizing these structures.

HOW THE GLOBAL RULES CONSTRAIN NATIONS

Many of the evils that are often attributed to capitalism are actually the consequences of those global arrangements that place tight restrictions on what governments are able to do. This was most obvious with the classical gold standard system, from 1880 to 1914. The idea of combining the gold standard with free trade meant globalizing the most extreme form of laissez-faire, so that governments would have no choice but to keep their hands off the market. Since we have shown that separating government from the market is impossible, the actual project was to prevent governments from doing anything to assist those with the least bargaining power in the marketplace, specifically working people and the poor. The gold standard exerted pressure on governments to sit on their hands as hunger and deprivation rose because any increase in government outlays risked the additional problems that came with running a budget deficit. Similarly, if a dramatic rise in cheap foreign agricultural imports threatened to ruin farmers, government was again expected to remain on the sidelines.[17]

To be sure, the gold standard often did not actually function as the theory suggested. Once governments recognized the destructive consequences of gold outflows, they found a number of subtle mechanisms to avert the downward spiral. If subtle techniques did not work, they would usually try to head off difficulties by increasing their foreign borrowing to tide them through a difficult period in their international accounts. But this strategy was also risky since a country might have difficulty keeping up the interest payments on its international debts. Then as now, the government would be forced to accept a painful dose of austerity as the price of renegotiating its foreign debts. This almost always involved accepting higher unemployment, lower wages, and cuts in government spending—the same results that would have been produced by an outflow of gold.

The combination of the gold standard and free trade made it extremely difficult for societies to enact cooperative relations with the expanding working class. Employers were reluctant to make any concessions on wages and working conditions for fear that foreign competitors who treated their employees even worse might gain an advantage. At the same time, the creation of old-age pensions, unemployment insurance, and other transfer programs that decreased economic insecurity both violated the laissez-faire spirit of the gold standard and risked either budget deficits or tax increases, which might generate a negative response by global investors.

Once the gold standard was replaced during World War II with a different international monetary system, there was a considerable relaxing of these constraints for most developed nations. This was the era of Bretton Woods (1945–1973), when governments used Keynesian tools to achieve full employment, oversaw a significant improvement in the standard of living of the industrial working class, and developed a wide range of transfer policies to reduce economic insecurity. In fact, two nations had already begun in the 1930s pursuing this direction— Sweden and the United States. In both cases, the new policy direction came only after the Swedish and U.S. governments had opted to abandon the gold standard.

But this period of relaxed global constraints did not last. The financial arrangements of the Bretton Woods era slid into crisis toward the end of the 1960s, and a global consensus on how they could be fixed was lacking. During the crisis of the Nixon presidency caused by Watergate, the U.S. and Europe reluctantly agreed to allow exchange rates to float freely on the market. Most of the key actors at the time saw this as a temporary solution until a better arrangement could be negotiated. But as the Watergate crisis deepened, such negotiations were postponed, and the temporary remedy became permanent. With floating exchange rates came much greater volatility in the foreign exchange markets; large swings in the relative value of major currencies were increasingly common. These swings made it difficult for governments to enforce limits on international capital mobility since investors insisted that they be able to hedge against exchange rate risks by diversifying their currency portfolios. Yet, the freeing of capital mobility only further increased volatility in the currency markets.

It was this growing exchange rate volatility that drove the European Community to launch the European Exchange Rate Mechanism in 1979 to create greater stability among the European currencies. Resources were pooled so that countries could intervene in the foreign exchange market to keep their national currency from moving too high or too low relative to other currencies. But in 1992, when speculative pressure on the English pound intensified, the U.K. government was forced to devalue the pound and withdraw from the Exchange Rate Mechanism. Everyone recognized that currency speculators could make bets that were large enough to overwhelm governmental efforts to keep a currency within a particular range.

This was the context in which member states of the European Community began moving toward the creation of the euro as a common currency, officially launched in 1999. The introduction of the common currency instantly solved the problem of the potential fluctuation in the exchange rate between different currencies such as the Italian lira and the German mark. With both countries now using the euro, firms could enter into long-term contracts with no worries about exchange rate changes. In short, the decision to adopt a common currency was a way to insulate economic transactions within the Eurozone from the heightened volatility of international exchange rates.[18]

But in the aftermath of the global financial crisis in 2008, it became obvious that the design of the common currency zone was deeply flawed. There was no mechanism to allow for adjustment between nations within the zone that were experiencing different rates of growth and different rates of inflation, and the Eurozone also lacked the institutions required to support national banking systems that slid into crisis. European leaders in the 1990s had rushed into an incomplete common currency arrangement in order to escape the global exchange rate volatility that was threatening to disrupt tighter European economic integration.

The consequence is that, both within Europe and outside it, the world once again has a set of global economic rules that has reinstated many of the tight constraints of the gold standard era. Back in the gold standard era, the global financial architecture blocked governments from acting to protect workers and the poor from harsh economic downturns. Now it is international institutions such as the International Monetary Fund and the European Community that force governments to impose on their own people high rates of unemployment, hunger, and misery. Moreover, as the Greek case has demonstrated, this type of forced austerity does not work to stimulate an economic recovery. The Greek economy has remained well below its previous peak for eight years, with few signs of economic recovery.[19]

Yet Greece is just the most dramatic case of a much more widespread phenomenon. In 2009, there was a broad global consensus among political leaders that drastic actions were needed to prevent the global economy from sliding into a severe depression. Governments around the world were encouraged to engage in massive deficit spending to stimulate their economies, and the International Monetary Fund took the unprecedented step of adding close to $250 billion in global stimulus by adding that sum to each nation's IMF reserves. These efforts succeeded in stopping the global economy's slide into depression. It seemed for a moment that the world had learned the lesson of the 1930s, which is that governments and international institutions have the necessary tools to prevent a global depression and restart global growth.

But almost as soon as it became clear that a slide into depression had been halted, the consensus in favor of stimulus disappeared. In 2010, the world's major nations turned toward austerity.[20] The idea was that if a nation balanced its government budget, private investment would accelerate and produce a new spurt of economic growth. This has not worked to restart growth, but with floating exchange rates and freely moving capital, any nation that tries to use government stimulus will quickly be punished with speculative pressure against its currency. Governments very quickly learned the lesson and recognized that enacting any form of stimulus was extremely risky; the safest thing to do was to announce the government's determination to balance its budget even if that meant considerable hardship for the population. This is part of the reason why the recovery from the 2008–2009 economic crisis has been so slow.[21] When nations with faster growth are at risk of being penalized by speculative pressure against their currencies, the world economy gets locked into a pattern of slow growth. Within the existing architecture, there is no obvious way to overcome this bias.

THE POSSIBILITIES OF CHANGE

There are, however, real alternatives to the current global economic rules. Just as there was a shared decision in the 1940s to create a system that was different from the gold standard, so it is possible now to create a new set of rules that would eliminate many of the negative features of the current global order. Three particular changes could make a huge difference both in stabilizing the global economy and in opening up political space within national economies.

First, the dollar's role as the central international currency should gradually be phased out in favor of an internationally created currency. This was the idea that John Maynard Keynes proposed in the 1940s.[22] The creation of an institution that is equivalent to a global central bank would make it possible to adjust the supply of international money to adapt to changing global economic conditions. If the world were sliding into recession, the pace of monetary creation would accelerate, and it could be slowed when the global economy was in danger of overheating. This step would both eliminate the deflationary bias of the current arrangements and force the United States to bring its international accounts into balance.

Second, there would be a very significant expansion in the channeling of credit through nonprofit international institutions to finance economic and social development in the less-developed nations of the world. In recent decades, capital has generally been flowing from the poorer nations to the richer nations—a trend that makes narrowing the gap between developed and developing nations virtually impossible. Channeling a growing share of capital through these nonprofit intermediaries would both improve the allocation of capital and protect developing nations from short-term capital flows that could be quickly reversed.

Third, specific measures are needed to reduce the volatility of exchange rates and slow down global capital movements. This step would likely involve a movement back to a fixed exchange rate regime and the use of the global financial transaction tax to discourage speculative transactions. These steps combined with the ability of governments to rely on short-term assistance from an institution similar to a global central bank would ideally expand the policy autonomy of individual governments, so they would be able to build inclusive and cooperative national economies.[23]

The big question is, what are the actual chances of bringing about these reforms of the global economic rules in the near future? Increasingly sophisticated global social movements have been able to win real reforms at the global level. Since the 1970s, environmentalists have pushed for global agreements to outlaw destructive environmental practices. For the last three decades, these efforts have focused on trying to slow the buildup of greenhouse gases that drives global climate change. The UN climate change initiative that began with the Kyoto Protocol in 1997 has been widely criticized as insufficient and ineffective, but stronger global efforts are under way. A meaningful global agreement was reached at the United Nations Climate Change Conference, which took place in Paris in late 2015. Recent data on the growth of renewable energy capacity across the globe has made it more likely that the global community will agree to leave significant deposits of coal and oil underground and untouched.

Social movement pressures have already impacted some of the rules governing international economic transactions. For example, up through the 1990s, the spread of HIV/AIDS in Africa continued unabated because governments could simply not afford the cost of the antiviral drugs that had proven effective against the epidemic in developed nations. However, since then, social movement pressures have led to a dramatic increase in the availability of these medications. One mechanism is the 2001 Doha declaration, signed at the WTO ministerial meeting, which gave governments expanded rights to prioritize public health over intellectual property rights. A second mechanism is a significant expansion in public and private initiatives to finance the increased availability of critical medicines through efforts such as the President's Emergency Plan for AIDS Relief (PEP-FAR) and the Gates Foundation.

Social movement pressures have also been successful in defeating a number of major global trade initiatives. In the late 1990s, protest activity led to the tabling of the Multilateral Agreement on Investing, which would have enshrined new protections for international investors. In the early 2000s, mobilizations across Latin America succeeded in derailing the Free Trade Area of the Americas. Grassroots organizing also led to the defeat of the Trans-Pacific Partnership, and a similar fate is likely for the Transatlantic Trade and Investment Partnership.

These successes have not been limited to blocking actions. Global activists have prioritized the creation of a global financial transaction tax that would be imposed on foreign exchange transactions. The idea is that even a very small tax of .001 percent would significantly increase transaction costs for currency speculators, and that would dampen some of the excessive volatility in these markets. With less exchange rate volatility and higher transaction costs, international capital movements would slow down, and that would give policy makers greater room to maneuver.[24] The idea did reach the agenda of the Group of Twenty in the years after the global financial crisis. Moreover, the imposition of such a tax on all financial transactions was actually approved by the European Parliament in 2012, although continuing controversy has postponed any steps toward actual implementation.

Global social movements organized to reshape the global economic rules have a unique opportunity because global discontent with the existing system is very strong. Many governments are already on record as favoring major reforms of the global order. Discontent among the less-developed nations has smoldered for years because the opportunities for development have been so limited under the current system.

Dissatisfaction with the global order has reached a whole new level with China actively building alliances to challenge the current dollar-centered global monetary system. Moreover, China launched the Asian Infrastructure Bank against the open opposition of the United States. The challenge posed by the Chinese is particularly acute because the traditional allies of the United States—Japan and the European Community—have their own deep reasons for discontent with the dollar-centered global economy. Japan has been repeatedly whipsawed by huge changes in the dollar-yen exchange rate, which exacerbates Japan's already serious problems of a shrinking population and insufficient consumer demand.

The case of the European Community is complicated because of the intense internal conflict between the German and Dutch advocates of balanced budgets and austerity and those who favor more economic stimulus to produce faster growth in the entire Eurozone. These divisions came to a head in the intense conflict over a third aid package for Greece in June and July of 2015. But as both factions advance proposals to heal the divisions within the Eurozone, it should become apparent that reform of European institutions would be far easier to accomplish within the framework of a reformed set of global economic rules. If, for example, the U.S. were constrained from running endless current account deficits, if the rapid movement of short-term capital flows across the global economy were slowed, if exchange rate volatility were dampened, and if there were tighter constraints on the global lending of banks in the U.S. and the U.K., it would become substantially easier for Europe to find a way to make the Eurozone sustainable.

Finally, there is the question of the United States itself. For the last forty years, the U.S. has strenuously resisted efforts to reform the global economic rules on the lines suggested here. On the contrary, the U.S. has fought intensely to defend and extend the status quo, with ever more global agreements that protect corporate intellectual property and investor rights. The U.S. has also shown few signs of retreating from its extensive global military commitments, including 662 overseas military bases in thirty-eight countries. In fact, the ever-expanding battle against Islamic extremists has extended U.S. military reach even further than during the Cold War period.

Nevertheless, there are signs that some parts of the U.S. elite recognize the inevitability of a U.S. retreat from its overextended global stance. Even if the elite faction in the U.S. that opposes any retreat from global empire remains dominant, it is highly uncertain what would happen if the U.S. were challenged by a powerful global social movement that had the support of key national governments. Both the U.S. government and its most powerful businesses have a strong incentive to offer compromises when they face determined challenges from global reform coalitions. Intransigent resistance to change would diminish the legitimacy of the existing order and lead more nations to bend or break the existing rules. Faced with a potential slide into global anarchy, the U.S. would be likely to make concessions.

A critical lesson from studies of national politics is that social movements are most likely to have a significant impact when there are divisions within the existing elites. When elites are unified, they can counter pressures from below by combining small and symbolic concessions with repression. But when movements are able to exacerbate divisions within the elite, they are more likely to win significant concessions or even set in motion processes that transform the existing order.

To be sure, one should not minimize the difficulties in mobilizing a powerful global social movement to change the rules of the global economic system. Building alliances transnationally presents both logistical and linguistic challenges and the need to bridge longstanding divisions. For example, cooperation among activists from developed and developing nations, whether the issue is the environment, intellectual property, or global financial regulation, must overcome high levels of mistrust. Social movements in the developing world are understandably fearful that the well-funded organizations from richer nations would dominate the coalition and that whatever victories are won would do little to address the structured inequalities of the global economy. And even when such unity can be forged, building alliances of convenience with governments or sympathetic business groups adds a whole range of tactical and strategic challenges.

The point remains that the global economic rules have been a key element in reinforcing the class power of the owning class globally, and those rules could be changed by global social movement pressures. Different rules would undermine that class power and make it more feasible to achieve greater economic equality, more cooperative employment systems, and more effective democratic governance.[25]

CONCLUSION

Mobilizing a transnational social movement to reform the rules governing the global economy is not just needed on the grounds of social and economic fairness; it is also needed for human survival. Our ability to avoid environmental catastrophe requires new global rules that will assure that vast reserves of coal and oil are kept in the ground. But global peace also requires new political structures and agreements to create and maintain global order. It is a myth that every nation embracing markets and profits will automatically produce global harmony. On the contrary, as nations pursue their advantage in global economic competition, the result can be dangerous global rivalries, intensified nationalism, and open warfare. The failure to understand that global order must be created through politics can lead to a replay of the rise of fascism in the 1930s.

But this is difficult to see when one thinks that capitalism involves a set of unchanging structures that make it impossible for a society to move toward greater equality and deeper democracy. As I argued earlier, the historical data on income and wealth inequality assembled by Thomas Piketty and his colleagues shows very clearly that from 1914 to 1973, Western societies were in fact substantially less unequal. And under the international economic rules that were in effect from 1945 to 1973, these steps toward greater equality were sustained. In short, what some call capitalism has been in continuous flux, and there are no unchanging structures that inevitably limit our choices in the present.

This widely propagated claim about unchanging structures helps us to understand why discussions of alternatives to the global status quo continue to be so impoverished. Margaret Thatcher boastfully asserted that "there is no alternative" to the kind of free market capitalism that she espoused, and while legions of analysts and activists have railed against her claim, the fact is that she won that particular war. The proof is in the response to the near collapse of the global economy in 2008 and 2009. Yes, the severity of the global financial crisis produced much intense debate over alternatives for perhaps a year, but then the discussion fizzled out. Even when activism reemerged in the Occupy Wall Street movement, there was a brief flowering of utopian longings, but very little in the way of concrete alternatives to the status quo. Since then, even eight long years after the global crisis first broke out, there has been almost no discussion of a fundamental overhaul of the global economic order.

The reality is that the institutions of the global economy have been rebuilt repeatedly since the beginning of the nineteenth century. Another such rebuilding is urgently needed because the existing global economy is badly broken. It is responding far too slowly to the imperative to cut greenhouse gases to protect the earth from climate change. It is blocking real economic development in many parts of the Global South with the consequence of more and more failed states and an ever-rising number of global refugees fleeing homelands that provide neither safety nor livelihoods. It is vulnerable to yet more dangerous financial bubbles as vast amounts of mobile capital act like lemmings in pursuit of higher returns. And most fundamentally, it has been unable to bring down elevated levels of global unemployment or reverse the concentration of income and wealth in the hands of a global oligarchy, and this failure fuels the rise of populist and authoritarian movements.

CHAPTER SEVEN

Beyond Illusions

It is unrealistic to imagine that people will stop using the term "capitalism"—no matter how strong the arguments against the term might be. But my hope is to make people think when they hear or read the term about the various illusions that are now associated with the word. Three of these illusions are particularly important. The first is the often-repeated but false claim that we cannot fix the environment, fix the extreme inequalities in the distribution of income and wealth, or eliminate poverty without undermining the prosperity that a market economy has generated. Such assertions rest on false claims about the autonomy of the market system and a failure to understand that markets themselves require restraints on the pursuit of self-interest.

Such claims often use the language of the perversity thesis, arguing that well-intentioned measures such as the minimum wage, programs to assist the poor, and a variety of government regulations are bound to have perverse consequences because they interfere with the ability of the price mechanism to produce the optimal use of economic inputs.[1] But once we discard the idea of the market economy as an autonomous entity standing on its own, it follows that these perverse consequences are not inevitable.

In fact, there is something like a reverse perversity mechanism at work in market economies. Right-wing efforts to eliminate consumer-friendly and employee-friendly regulations encourage businesses to make profits by imposing costs on consumers, employees, or others. Supreme Court decisions that equate money and speech, striking down limits on campaign contributions, push the economy in the direction of oligarchy by expanding the political influence of entrenched business interests. Oligarchy actually undermines economic dynamism since firms that are effectively protected from competition have little incentive to invest or innovate.

The second key illusion is that efforts to transform the way that a market economy works are doomed to failure because they are inconsistent with capitalism's basic DNA. This has been the right's favorite argument against any reform measures that seek to reshape markets to protect the environment or reduce inequality. This illusion can be dispelled by simply looking at how much change has occurred over the last two hundred years in societies where much economic activity continues to be organized around the pursuit of profit. Developed societies have transitioned from rule by elites to a system of mass democracy. There has been a spectacular growth in the size and reach of government, and the education level of the population increased dramatically. Who knows what further changes might occur over the next hundred years as society is reorganized around the production of human habitation.

In the United States, that two-hundred-year history has been marked by periods of institutional discontinuity, when old structures of power were broken apart and distinctly new arrangements were put in place. The most dramatic of these moments were the Civil War and the New Deal, but the Progressive Era and the 1960s also were significant reform epochs. Rather than thinking of U.S. history in terms of an unchanging capitalist order, it is important to see that these various reform epochs have played a huge role in maintaining the economy's dynamism.

In fact, the United States is now long overdue for another one of these reform epochs. In the fifty years that have passed since the last reform epoch, our society has moved far down the road to oligarchy with extreme inequality of income and wealth and too much power in the hands of entrenched business enterprises that have insulated themselves from effective competition. The reality is exactly the opposite of the right's argument; if we are to continue to have a vibrant and productive economy, we have no choice but to use the political process to again reshape how markets work.

The third important illusion is the claim that there is no alternative because by definition capitalism entails an autonomous, self-regulating market. But in fact, there has never been an autonomous self-regulating market and there never will be, since government action is necessary to constitute a market system. Moreover, society is constantly reconstructing the market system, so there is always the alternative of choosing a mode of reconstruction that is more compatible with democracy, equality, and environmental sustainability. Realizing these alternatives, however, also requires restructuring the rules and institutions that govern the global economy. These arrangements can and do significantly constrain what options are available within particular societies. But global rules are not set in stone; they are also under constant negotiation and reconstruction. So there remains a genuine opportunity to link together a politics of reform at the national level with a politics of global reform that could work in synergy.

Discarding these illusions and embracing this reform project is urgent because we are living at a time when our existing economic arrangements—both domestically and globally—are so obviously failing. The most glaring failure is the very slow progress in meeting the challenge of climate change. The global community ignored the scientific warnings of potential catastrophe for decades, and the pace of action has only begun to accelerate as we are starting to see some of those prophecies fulfilled.

A second failure is the deteriorating economic conditions in large parts of the Global South. While the rise of China and India has pulled hundreds of millions of people out of poverty, the story is not so positive in much of the rest of Asia, Latin America, and Africa. In the post-2008 era of slower economic growth in the rich nations, many nations in the developing world have been going backward. The added pressures of climate change have resulted in dramatic increases in violence and economic hardship, leading in turn to an ever-expanding global population of refugees desperate to reach the relative safety of North America, Europe, or Australia. Tens of thousands of people are willing to rely on small boats to cross the Mediterranean from Africa to Europe or to cross the Andaman Sea from Burma to Indonesia, and thousands of others face the dangers of crossing miles of desert to get into the U.S. from Mexico. For every person who embarks on these risky journeys, there are hundreds or thousands more who share the same desperation.

The refugee crisis and the growing number of failed states around the world indicate the difficulties many developing nations face in providing much of their populations with stable or improving life chances. Part of the problem is that nations cannot compete in the current world economy without computers, smart phones, software, and internet access, but virtually all of this apparatus must be imported from already-developed nations. So the IT revolution acts as a kind of tax on whatever foreign exchange nations in the Global South are able to earn. But earnings from agricultural exports and raw materials have been falling in real terms, and most poor countries also have to import cars, trucks, machinery, and most other manufactured goods. The current global trade regime also keeps governments from protecting homegrown firms that try to compete with products made in the rich nations. As a consequence, literally hundreds of millions of people have been forced into the least productive forms of employment, such as selling on the street or farming tiny plots of land.

The third failure is the chronically weak performance of the developed economies in the years since the global financial crisis. Europe and Japan have constantly teetered on the edge of recession; the United States has done slightly better thanks to aggressive action by the Federal Reserve to pump new money into the economy. But while unemployment in the United States has come down considerably, the percentage of adults in the labor force remains low by recent historical standards. The 62.6 percent adult participation rate in mid-2015 was the lowest level since 1977, when the entrance of married women into the labor force was just beginning to accelerate. In short, none of the richer nations have been able to create enough decent-paying jobs to produce the kind of broadly shared prosperity that they had experienced in earlier decades.

Moreover, there is little hope that this situation will improve any time soon. Key elites in Europe and the U.S. have a strong preference for continued austerity policies, and they have consistently defeated renewed efforts to jump-start economic activity with more public-sector spending. Their mantra since 2010 has been that public-sector budget tightening will create increased confidence in the private sector, and this will bring forth heightened levels of private investment. That this has not happened for eight long years does not appear to diminish enthusiasm for this policy choice.

Continued austerity policies mean that the global economy faces the threat of another potential catastrophic economic downturn that could destroy what little remains of a system of global order. The period of slow growth since 2010 has already seen heightened geopolitical conflicts across the Middle East, on the borders of Russia, and in the South China Sea. Within Europe itself, previously marginalized right-wing anti-immigrant parties have gained greater electoral traction even in the largest nations of the European Community. With another serious global economic slowdown, it is not difficult to anticipate a dramatic escalation of global tensions and heightened influence by political parties committed to extreme nationalism and ethnic exclusion. With these pressures, it will become ever more difficult to organize cooperative global efforts to restart the world economy.

WHY THE COMPLACENCY?

These dramatic failures of current global arrangements should have generated an intense international debate about what needs to be done to restructure the current global order. And yet, that discussion is not taking place. Yes, there are ongoing conversations about how to respond to climate change, the global refugee crisis, financial regulation, the chaos in the Middle East, and the rise of China, but very rarely are these issues linked to the poor performance of the global economy in the post-2008 period.

To be sure, many ordinary people around the world are aware that something is terribly wrong and they have mobilized in various ways to demand change. Sustained mass demonstrations have occurred from Cairo to Kiev to Hong Kong, sometimes even forcing a change in government. In many places, voters are abandoning mainstream political parties and giving their votes to protest parties of the left, the right, and the center. In the United States, we have seen the unprecedented election of Donald Trump.

Yet much of the political elite in the U.S. and abroad still does not grasp that status quo policies are no longer working. They ignore mass protests and electoral support for anti-establishment parties and candidates on the assumption that these insurgencies will ultimately die out, as many of them do. Nowhere has this been clearer than in the European Community's dealing with Greece's left-wing Syriza government in 2015. Instead of seeing the election of a recently created far-left party as an indication that the Greek public must be desperate for change, they interpreted it as a foolish electoral error by a misguided population.

Why are these global political elites so clueless and so determined to stick with their embrace of austerity as the solution to virtually all problems? They are trapped within the illusion that capitalism is an unchanging and coherent global structure that must be respected at all costs. To be sure, their surrender to this illusion is reinforced on a daily basis by pressures from two connected directions. First, the global financial markets are ready to punish political leaders who might violate market orthodoxy. Second, those with great wealth insist that no alternatives to the status quo can even be contemplated.

While both of these sources of pressure are formidable, they are not definitive by themselves. The job of political elites is to figure out how to work around various constraints in order to maintain as much political support as possible. Ordinarily, when public support starts to slip away, political elites begin to improvise new policies that are designed to hold on to that support. But ever since the downturn of the global economy was halted in 2009, such improvisation on key issues of economic policy has been extremely rare. Sure, political leaders try to rebuild support by taking on other issues such as reducing immigration, supporting anti-terrorism policies, or acting more aggressively toward their neighbors. But they have basically steered clear of dealing with the fundamental weaknesses of the global economy.

The freedom of action of national leaders to develop new policy directions is quite limited because we now have a global set of rules that emulates the old gold standard in discouraging experimentation at the national level. But this only shifts the question. Why haven't these political leaders convened emergency global meetings to restructure the rules of the global economy so that they are able to experiment boldly and solve their domestic economic problems? Here again, the only plausible explanation is that they are convinced that capitalism gives them no way out. Our political leaders are being held hostage by the illusion that we live within a coherent, unified, and unchangeable capitalist order.

A SMALL DETOUR: CONFRONTING THE GROWTH ISSUE

This book has treated economic dynamism as a good thing when it is focused on using resources efficiently to produce more and better products without imposing costs on employees, consumers, or the environment. However, strong voices are now arguing that this historic fixation on economic growth is destroying the planet and that we should pursue "de-growth" instead.[2] Advocates of de-growth have a point since continued growth along the lines of the last two centuries is impossible and unsustainable. But the theorists of de-growth fail to understand that it is possible to have enhanced human well-being without the kind of resource-destroying growth that has been typical through the industrial era.

The issue can be clarified by distinguishing between quantitative growth and qualitative growth.[3] Quantitative growth has been pursued since the Industrial Revolution; it means more physical output and more resources used. Qualitative growth is resource conserving; it involves meeting human needs without increasing the burden on the planet. When we spend money to clean up polluted rivers or to develop technologies that allow us to make use of recycled materials, we are pursuing qualitative growth.

Many countries have already started the transition to qualitative growth. This is part of the emergence of an economy organized around the production of human habitation. One indicator is the changing nature of consumption. It used to be that most consumer purchases were goods that required using up vast amounts of material. For example, seventy years ago, food made up almost 33 percent of an average family's budget. Now, however, most of our consumption is made up of services, and many of those services are far less resource intensive than goods production. Education and health care, for example, comprise almost 30 percent of our economy, but they place far less strain on the environment than a steel mill or auto plant. At the same time, we have made our goods production considerably less resource intensive. The amount of land required for our farms has fallen sharply, and the amount of energy used to produce a dollar's worth of economic output has also fallen substantially.

But while this transition is already under way, the pace of the transition is far too slow to solve our environmental and economic problems. The slow pace can be traced to existing policies and mind-sets that continue to be biased in favor of quantitative growth. The bias is most obvious in our economic statistics. The removal of mountaintops to increase coal production counts as increased output, but the GDP does not measure the value of clean water and clean air. Similarly, the value of improved health for the elderly, more effective education, increased leisure time, jobs that are more satisfying, greater economic security, and living in more attractive neighborhoods is not directly measured in our economic output statistics.

In short, policies that truly prioritize qualitative growth would make it possible to produce substantially more human satisfaction while economizing on the key economic inputs such as raw materials, energy, labor, and physical capital. De-growth advocates are mistaken in thinking of a steady-state economy on the output side rather than on the input side. We can get to a steady state where the inputs that are used up in production are stable or actually declining, but that hardly means that we have to make do with exactly the same amount of economic output. On the contrary, the idea is to mobilize human ingenuity so that we can produce higher levels of human satisfaction with less use of resources while also making progress in reversing damage to the planet.

The qualitative growth concept also makes room for the urgent task of providing more resources to the world's poorest people. To be sure, this makes the environmental challenge even greater since it is necessary to reduce greenhouse gases at the same time that energy use per capita in the Global South rises toward Western levels. But it is morally unacceptable to address climate change by telling the global poor that they must continue to make do with far fewer resources. A combination of renewable energy technologies and global redistributive measures would make this a feasible project.

But once the issue of feasibility is raised, a key question emerges. Is a full transition to qualitative growth possible in an economy where the profit motive is still a powerful force? This brings us back to where this book began: what do people mean when they invoke the concept of capitalism? In the conventional view, capitalism means endless economic growth. It is an inherently dynamic system that is constantly providing new goods and services. To be sure, this endless growth is also punctuated by periodic economic downturns. In this conventional view, the pursuit of profit is inherently incompatible with an economy that achieves some type of steady state.

My view is that through the exercise of political will, exerted both at the national and the global level, the pursuit of profit could be directed to produce an economy that provides ever-growing outputs with constant or falling inputs. The fuel efficiency standards for automobiles are a useful metaphor here. Periodically, the U.S. Congress increases the average fuel efficiency requirements for the cars produced by the various automakers. When the standards were first imposed in 1975, they mandated an average of 18 miles per gallon. By 2011, the goal was 30.2 miles per gallon, and by 2025, the target is 46–60 miles per gallon depending on the size of the car. It is expected that these targets will force auto companies to increase their production of zero emission vehicles.

The idea is to channel the corporate pursuit of profit into figuring out how to achieve these goals. Managers have to assemble teams of engineers to produce more efficient engines, find lighter materials, and experiment with more radical innovations. To be sure, as with any regulatory scheme, there have been glitches such as Volkswagen's cynical strategy of cheating on its diesel emissions. Nevertheless, the trajectory over time suggests that this approach can be effective. The use of petroleum in the U.S. transportation sector peaked at 27.5 trillion BTUs in 2006 and fell to 25.7 in 2016—a decline of 6.5 percent in ten years.[4] Of course, much more rapid progress is needed to respond to global climate change, but there is evidence that these regulatory tools can work.

Since part of qualitative growth is creating more economic security and better jobs, one might imagine using a parallel regulatory mechanism to push businesses to improve their employment conditions. A score card that would be maintained by an independent nonprofit could look at such variables as mobility opportunities, wage levels, employee health and safety, opportunities for employee voices to be heard, and so on. Firms that earned As on the report card might then be eligible for a reduction in their tax bill, while those who earned Cs or below would be required to pay a tax penalty. In sum, the logic of maximizing after-tax profits could be used to improve employees' experience at work. Again, employers will figure out ways to game the system and earn rewards that are not really merited, but regular monitoring and reevaluation could defeat these evasive moves, and firms would make actual improvements in working conditions.

In short, the profit mechanism can work to reward individuals or firms for figuring out innovative ways to meet human needs in ways that are efficient and resource conserving. There are, however, several important qualifications. Individuals or firms who engage in predatory action or who figure out inefficient and wasteful paths to profitability should not be rewarded. Also, those who are earning profits must be blocked from exerting political influence that they could use to extract disproportionate profits and rewards for unproductive actions. Finally, it seems likely that the total weight of profit-oriented activity in the economy will probably continue to decline as the role of nonprofit economic institutions expands.

THINKING ABOUT ALTERNATIVES

If our political leaders were not trapped in the illusions of capitalism, they would understand that the problems of the world economy today are remarkably similar to those of the 1930s. Then and now, the world economy's capacity to produce goods and services vastly exceeds available purchasing power. In the 1930s, that gap took the form of too much production, particularly in U.S. farms and factories. The glut of agricultural products was dramatized by the slaughter and burial of six million surplus pigs in 1933, at a time when hunger was widespread in Europe and other parts of the world.[5] Today, the gap takes the form of the "global glut of saving" that was identified by former Federal Reserve chief Ben Bernanke.[6] Millions of newly middle-class people in Asia are accumulating saving that exceed the supply of good investment instruments currently available in the world economy. Leading up to 2008, Wall Street responded to this shortage by expanding the supply of risky mortgage-based bonds, pretending these were safe investment instruments.

What does it mean to say that there is an insufficient supply of good investment instruments? Big corporations, not just in the United States but around the world, are able to finance most of their new investments out of profits. Their need to raise money in the capital markets by selling equities or bonds is small relative to the total amount of global saving. These corporations are being understandably cautious; they do not see big increases in demand happening in either the developed nations or the developing ones. They are not about to borrow new capital to expand output when the demand for additional goods and services is unlikely to materialize.

But, of course, this has nothing to do with actual need. In the U.S., for example, just repairing the nation's physical infrastructure is estimated to cost more than $4.6 trillion over the next decade, and there are millions of people who would be happy to move out of substandard housing into better buildings and better neighborhoods.[7] Moreover, around the world, there are at least 2.2 billion people living in extreme poverty who are in need of all kinds of goods and services. But corporations can only respond to needs that come with purchasing power. They cannot make profits by giving away things to the global poor.

So in today's crisis, we do not need to kill a lot of surplus pigs or manage huge inventories of unsold products. Corporations have become very sophisticated about matching production to actual demand so they avoid the accumulation of excess inventory. The crisis manifests as a global saving glut, or vast pools of money that are not able to find productive uses. This is what lies behind the long period of historically low interest rates that began with the emergency efforts to avoid a global depression in 2008 and 2009.

Some have argued that the proper response to low interest rates and a global saving glut is for governments to increase their borrowing and use the proceeds to build and rebuild infrastructure, accelerate the movement away from fossil fuels, and respond to the needs of the global poor by providing housing, education, health care, and basic government services. This has not happened, however. Instead, since 2010, the global advocates of austerity have prevailed and have insisted that governments actually reduce their borrowing. Moreover, any government that tries to defy this wisdom experiences speculative pressure against its currency, its government debt, and its banking institutions. Thus far, pretty much every nation has succumbed to this pressure and joined the austerity club.

But this is precisely where the lessons of the crisis of the 1930s have been forgotten. There was no spontaneous, market-driven recovery from the Great Depression led by business decisions to increase investment. On the contrary, in most countries, significant recovery did not happen until nations began military spending to re-arm for World War II. But if military spending was needed for a return to full employment, how did the world economy avoid a return to depression conditions at the end of World War II? What measures made possible the three decades of dramatic economic growth from 1945 to 1975?

Four basic innovations together ramped up global demand to eliminate the shortfall of the depression years. First, in the developed nations, deliberate policies worked to enhance the purchasing power of people in the bottom half of the income distribution. In the U.S., the increases in the percentage of the labor force represented by unions combined with a government commitment to full employment and progressive taxation made possible enhanced purchasing power for households that had previously been very limited in their consumption. In Europe, the same thing happened, but the mechanism tended to be increased government outlays for public services.

Second, pretty much everywhere, there was dramatic growth in the size of government relative to the whole economy. A permanently higher level of public expenditures boosted demand in the economy, and certain government outlays, such as those for unemployment insurance and welfare, increased automatically in times of recession to push the economy back toward expansion. In Europe, a very substantial share of these increased government outlays went to public services such as health care and housing that particularly benefited those in the bottom half of the income distribution. In the U.S., starting in 1950, a large portion of government expenditures were used for national defense, and these heightened military expenditures strengthened economic demand.

Third, the U.S., in particular, relied on a tremendous expansion of consumer credit to strengthen demand for housing, cars, home furnishings, and later, higher education. This did not just happen; it was the outcome of government measures that created a network of new private financial institutions supported with government guarantees. The result was a major historical innovation, the creation of a mass consumption economy in which all but the poorest households had access to credit at what were usually manageable rates. This model was eventually adapted to many countries in Europe and East Asia and there, as well, it helped bring supply and demand into balance.

Finally, under U.S. leadership, there was a vast expansion in global credit to strengthen purchasing power in other parts of the world. In the immediate post–World War II period, there was the Marshall Plan, extensive U.S. military assistance, and expanded foreign investment by U.S.-based firms that helped Europe and Japan rebuild their economies. Over time, this was supplemented by the flow of credit to developing nations through foreign aid, bank lending, and sovereign debt issues. To be sure, these flows of credit were periodically interrupted by debt crises in which governments were required to embrace austerity, but the long-term trajectory has been ever higher levels of indebtedness by foreign governments, foreign firms, and average citizens.

The current predicament of the global economy is that the world economy needs more debt because debt is the fuel that drives demand. Without the capacity to borrow, global demand will be weak, new investments will not be undertaken, and the world will suffer an ongoing saving glut. But the debt that grows needs to be primarily good debt; there has to be a reasonable probability that borrowers will be able to keep up their payments on the debt burden that they have taken on. In a world where a disproportionate share of the growth in income goes to the top 1 percent of households, though, this condition cannot be met. When people's real incomes are stagnant or falling, those in the bottom half of the income distribution cannot afford to take on additional debt. Similarly, when developing economies are not gaining an adequate share of global income, their borrowing becomes unsustainable.

We should have learned from the 2008 crisis what happens when a significant share of the expanding debt is bad debt. Mortgage lending in the U.S. expanded very dramatically as the price of single-family homes in both good neighborhoods and bad rose at a completely unsustainable pace. When the housing bubble broke and millions of households suddenly owed more than their houses were actually worth, that accumulated debt turned into toxic sludge. And that sludge on the balance sheet of banks around the world was sufficient to create the worst financial crisis since the 1930s. Moreover, if past history is any guide, the same thing could keep happening. In the absence of good debt instruments, funds are likely to flow into speculative and unreliable debt issues.[8]

LESSONS FOR NOW

Two conclusions follow from this history. First, the world needs a lot more good debt as the fuel to keep the global economic engine working. Good debt is the mechanism through which demand can keep up with expanding global output so that enough jobs are created for the world's population. But the world's debt burden can only be sustainably increased with a more equal distribution of global income. This means that both within nations and between nations, there must be redistributive measures that provide ordinary people with sustained income flows so they can borrow to acquire houses, upgrade their skills, and invest in their children.

In a moment, we will address the mechanisms needed to redistribute income. But how do we go about assuring that the process of creating new debt is sustainable and avoids the periodic asset price bubbles and financial meltdowns of the recent past? The answer is that expanding the supply of credit is a public task; it cannot be done by the market acting on its own. In fact, when private banks create credit, they are able to do so only because there is a central bank that assures that their paper is treated as cash even if the bank is in trouble. In other words, credit creation is a public activity that the government allows private banks to perform as a kind of franchise.[9]

If credit creation is a public function, it follows that we need to find ways to expand the credit available in the global economy without exacerbating two current problems. The first is the familiar tendency of profit-oriented financial institutions to take on too much risk. When they are put in charge of creating credit, the danger is great that they will finance asset price bubbles that will come crashing down with disastrous consequences. The second is the widespread concern that central governments should be careful about taking on levels of sovereign debt that are too high relative to GDP. While I think that these fears of excessive government indebtedness are exaggerated, there is still an obvious need for a greater supply of good debt beyond the sovereign debt of nations.

One solution is John Maynard Keynes's proposal in the 1940s for the International Clearing Union as the central mechanism of the international monetary system. Keynes's idea was that the ability to increase the supply of international liquidity should be lodged in a global institution. This global institution would create a currency called "bancor," and, just as central banks do, the International Clearing Union could increase the supply of bancor at the appropriate rate to keep the global economy expanding at a desirable speed. The new issues of bancor would show up as part of the currency reserves of national governments and would make possible the expansion of the supply of credit within nations. Keynes's idea could also help address the problem of global inequality since the annual or semi-annual allocation of bancor could be tilted in favor of the poorest nations so they could grow their economies at a more rapid pace than middle-income and rich nations.

There is evidence to indicate that a bancor system could work. Back in 1969, the International Monetary Fund created special drawing rights, which are essentially the same thing as bancor— an internationally created mechanism to enhance each nation's international currency reserves. SDR allocations were made up through 1977, and then the instrument went into a thirty-year period of neglect. However, in 2009, as proposed by the U.S., the International Monetary Fund allocated $250 billion in SDRs as part of the effort to halt the slide of the global economy into depression. The mechanism worked exactly as intended; the addition to their reserves encouraged governments to pursue expansionary policies, and those reversed the global downturn.

Another mechanism for expanding the supply of global credit also has a track record of success and only needs to be scaled up to assure that global supply and demand could be brought into balance. This is the provision of credit through international institutions such as the World Bank, which sells bonds to investors around the world and uses the proceeds to finance development projects in different parts of the world. The entities that ultimately receive the loans and are responsible for repayment are often not central governments, but lower levels of government, private entities, or some kind of hybrid authority. While the World Bank's lending practices and priorities have been broadly criticized for their lack of sensitivity to the environment and to democratic input, the bank has proven over seven decades the viability of its financing model. It has been able to make loans to the poorest countries at subsidized interest rates, and it has produced steady returns to those who purchase its bonds.

A reformed World Bank along with a network of other global financing institutions would be able to scale up lending from $80 to $100 billion per year to $500 billion per year. Substantial parts of this funding could be addressed to the problem of climate change—financing clean energy production and energy conservation measures that are proven to be cost-effective. The funding could be channeled through public or private utilities or newly created energy authorities that would be able to pay down the loans with their enhanced capacity. Here again, much of the organizational infrastructure for this step is already in place. China has launched the Asia Infrastructure Bank, and as part of the United Nations Framework Convention on Climate Change, there is a Green Climate Fund that is close to operational. These entities, in combination with existing regional development banks, have the capacity to ramp up their operations to the scale that is needed.

Finally, at the national level, several countries have successfully experimented with public or quasi-public investment banks that finance infrastructure projects, provide funding for clean energy, and provide financing to promising firms that are advancing new technologies. The Brazilian National Development Bank and Germany's KfW are the best examples of such institutions, but many other countries have similar banks that operate on a smaller scale.

Ideally, these institutions are insulated from direct government interference, so their decisions are based on the quality of the project. They raise funds by selling bonds that are not counted as part of the nation's sovereign debt. But the way that they are structured assures that a very high percentage of the funds they raise in the capital markets is transformed into productive outlays that expand the total flow of goods and services. If this model were widely adopted, bond issues by these state development banks could absorb another large fraction of the global saving glut.

THE GLOBAL INEQUALITY PROBLEM

In sum, we know the institutional arrangements that could provide the high-quality debt needed for the world economy to absorb the goods and services that can be produced. But as mentioned earlier, these steps would fail without concerted efforts to reverse the current pattern, in which a very large share of global income goes to the top 1 percent of households. What is needed are powerful mechanisms to narrow the gap between rich nations and poor nations and between the poor and the rich within nations.

It is difficult for nations to change their position within the global hierarchy of wealth. Many of the success stories, like South Korea, China, and Brazil, have had very specific advantages that made it possible to leapfrog ahead of other nations. But now leapfrogging has become even more difficult because poorer nations are so heavily dependent on expensive, foreign-produced technologies that have become essential to life in the twenty-first century, including the smart phone, the computer, and the internet. While these technologies do enhance the capabilities of people in poor nations, they represent a huge burden on the limited foreign exchange that these nations are able to earn.

A first necessary step is to reverse the pattern of the last thirty years, in which capital has been flowing from poor nations to rich nations. As a consequence of past debt burdens or capital flight by the wealthy, most developing nations are not mobilizing their own domestic savings for expanding their own economies. Implementing the bancor plan and dramatically expanding lending by global development banks are critical steps for reversing this pattern and making more resources available for investment. Furthermore, developing nations should be encouraged to create state development banks that would channel resources into vital infrastructure projects.

Another necessary step is to reform the global trade and investment rules that have been institutionalized over the last thirty years because they have very substantially narrowed the policy space available to governments in developed nations. Governments need to be able to protect infant industries and erect barriers to the importing of expensive foreign luxury goods that drain valuable foreign exchange. The track record of those nations that have successfully industrialized since World War II show that their success would not have been possible without extensive state action, but many of these specific types of state action have been ruled out by various bilateral and multilateral agreements.

Yet another necessary step has become even more urgent as climate change brings drought, flooding, and other severely disruptive weather events. There needs to be a reliable mechanism that protects people from hunger and homelessness and supports their ability to adapt to a changing environment. The logical way to do this is by moving toward a global guaranteed income plan that provides everybody with enough income to survive hard times.[10] The size of the allotment would vary across nations, but the richer nations would contribute to support these payments in the world's poorest nations.

Movement toward a global income guarantee would help ameliorate many of the world's most intractable problems. It would put more purchasing power in the hands of low-income populations, and this would help stimulate economic development in poor neighborhoods and poor nations. It would also significantly strengthen the global community's resilience in the face of climate change. With the security of an income guarantee, people in low-lying areas would be more amenable to moving to higher ground. There would also be expected improvement in conservation efforts since poor people would no longer face difficult choices between starving or clearing forest land.

The income guarantee could also help ameliorate the global refugee crisis since those who are leaving their countries because of economic hardship would no longer face the same tragic choices.

Finally, implementing a global income guarantee could be a means to establish effective governance structures in those parts of the world that are plagued by failed governments and chronic civil war. The essential idea is that a global body, such as a United Nations agency, would have to come into these regions and begin setting up the infrastructure to administer the income guarantee. This infrastructure would then become the skeleton for rebuilding state institutions that are actually responsive to the interests of the area's people. While many foreign aid projects in the past have worked with this same idea of creating models of effective governance that could then be expanded, very few of them have focused on the critical task of providing the population with what people need the most—a guarantee of enough income to ensure their survival.

THE DOMESTIC INEQUALITY ISSUE

Some of these global measures could also help to reverse the trend toward rising inequality in the U.S. and other rich nations. Implementing a guaranteed income system would help to reverse the stagnation in compensation at the bottom of the labor market. People would no longer be forced to take the worst jobs with the worst working conditions for fear of being homeless and hungry. Those employers would have to upgrade both the pay and the working conditions. Moreover, as in the developing world, the increased purchasing power in low-income communities should help to drive economic development by creating new business opportunities.

Most of the other policies required to diminish wealth and income inequality are familiar because they existed and operated effectively at earlier times in U.S. history.[11] For example, tough anti-trust enforcement has been pursued in the past to prevent corporations from earning superprofits because the firm enjoys a monopoly or near monopoly. Since the Reagan administration, the government pursues such actions only in the most extreme cases and basically looks the other way when firms in highly concentrated industries collude to keep prices artificially high. Moreover, the evolution of laws around intellectual property has intensified the problem because the government is often in the position of enforcing the monopoly position of particular corporations. The most egregious example is the pharmaceutical industry, where firms routinely use their monopoly power to charge outrageous prices for their medications. But similar problems exist throughout the computer industry and providers of news, information, and entertainment. The balance that is supposed to exist between providing incentives for developing new content and having an open marketplace have been tilted much too far in the direction of winner-take-all profits.

Similarly, the U.S. tax code has been filled with loopholes and gaps that allow high-income individuals and corporations to avoid paying their fair share of taxes. The carried interest exemption, which allows hedge fund managers to be taxed at the capital gains rate, is so egregious that it has even been denounced by Donald Trump. But there are many other instances where the use of certain kinds of trusts or overseas tax havens has made a very significant dent in the revenue that the U.S. should collect. Apple and some of the other high-tech firms have negotiated private deals with certain governments to be able to route their profits in a way that minimizes their tax bills.

But while closing loopholes, raising rates, and tightening enforcement would bring in substantially more revenue, the U.S. also needs to institute the kind of broad-based consumption tax that has been a major revenue source for European governments. The reason is that the U.S. taxing structure is too dependent on payroll taxes for funding programs such as Social Security and Medicare. These high payroll taxes are a barrier to expanding employment, particularly at a time when there is a concerted effort to raise the minimum wage. It would be logical to combine incremental increases in the minimum wage with incremental reductions in these payroll taxes.

CONCLUSION

The theorists of a system called capitalism continually make the claim that the only way that society can enjoy prosperity is if all aspects of social life are dominated by the logic of profit maximizing. Their argument is that one cannot pick and choose; it is impossible to have highly productive business firms operating in an economy where the people, operating through their government, make decisions about how much inequality, how much pollution, and how much poverty their society will tolerate.

This is an illusion. The historical reality is that a society organized around self-regulating markets has never worked; every existing market society is actually a complex hybrid of market and nonmarket arrangements, as well as a delicate compromise between the pursuit of self-interest and restraints on that pursuit. So, in fact, we *can* pick and choose. We can reconstruct the market in a way that is consistent with the values of democracy, equality, and environmental sustainability. On the other side of the illusion lies a vast new world of possibilities.

Afterword

This afterword develops a brief critique of the way analysts and activists on the left continue to use the concept of capitalism. My main argument is that the term "capitalism" was effectively stolen by the right wing in the 1970s and 1980s and infused with a meaning that emphasizes capitalism's durability and its unchanging nature. So when those on the left use the term, they inadvertently reinforce the problematic claims of their political opponents. A similar episode of linguistic larceny happened earlier. Between 1890 and 1910, political thinkers in England and the United States effectively stole the term "liberalism" and redefined it from "economic liberalism" to "political liberalism."[1] This move was remarkably effective in weakening classical liberals, who favored limited government and greater reliance on markets. Moreover, when classical liberals insisted that their definition of the word was the proper one, nobody listened. Efforts by those on the left today who insist that they are defining capitalism correctly are doomed to similar futility.

But my argument is not simply a linguistic one. I also think that the term "capitalism," however it is defined, provides far less analytic leverage than people imagine. Here, I am building on the success and ultimate failure of the social science literature on the "varieties of capitalism" that flourished from the 1990s to about 2008.[2] Contributors to this body of literature began by arguing that even among those societies that could be defined as capitalist, there were significant variations in key institutions such as welfare systems, systems of corporate governance and financing, systems of employment relations, and innovation systems. The initial aspiration was to develop typologies that grouped countries into a relatively small number of types that shared common characteristics. The prototype for these efforts was Gosta Esping-Andersen's *Three Worlds of Welfare Capitalism*, which identified distinct types of public benefit systems among the developed nations.[3]

The "varieties of capitalism" project produced a stream of valuable studies that mapped significant variation across these developed market societies in institutions central to capitalism such as corporate ownership and employment relations.[4] But several problems emerged fairly quickly. First, it soon became apparent that it was difficult to fit all of the developed market societies into two or three major types; Japan and South Korea as well as Australia and New Zealand fit poorly into typologies rooted in Europe and North America.[5] Moreover, the typologies often did not line up across institutional arenas, and some countries kept changing their places within particular typologies—suddenly moving, for example, from a more social democratic welfare system to one that was more liberal, or developing a sophisticated, government-centered innovation system when it was classified in the type where government was disconnected from businesses.

Second, these typologies did not illuminate other critical aspects of social life in these countries. There is the important question of how different societies treat racial and ethnic minorities and recent immigrants. There is the issue of gender equality and how quickly or slowly different societies were moving to greater equality between men and women. There is the question of international relations and the extent to which particular nations are involved in exploitative relations with former colonies or other less-developed nations. And, of course, there is the issue of the strength and effectiveness of democratic institutions. The reality is that hardly anybody even tried to analyze these issues within the varieties of capitalism framework because it quickly became apparent that these other critical dimensions were not correlated with types of welfare systems or systems of employment relations.

One influential response to these problems was a shift from "varieties of capitalism" to the concept of "variegated capitalism."[6] This new terminology recognized that the project of developing a few major types was not viable and that one should expect huge variation in the institutional structures and social arrangements of existing capitalist societies. But in the concept of variegated capitalism, the word "capitalism" is doing relatively little work. It is simply suggesting that the variegation is occurring within a capitalist world economy that sets the limits on the types of variation that are possible.

THE GLOBAL DIMENSION

In this book, I have consistently argued that these global institutions do, in fact, play an extremely important role in constraining and limiting what is politically possible within national societies. In this respect, I agree with a focus on the global level that is suggested both by theorists of variegated capitalism and the world-systems perspective developed by Immanuel Wallerstein.[7] As argued in chapter 7, it is fundamentally important to focus on these global institutions and rules if one is to challenge the existing systems of inequality within and between nations.

World-system theory has been particularly important in showing the centrality of European imperial expansion in facilitating the initial breakthrough to modern economic growth in Northwest Europe. Rather than seeing colonialism, slavery, and racism as separate from economic development, they are recognized as playing a critical role in paving the way to the Industrial Revolution. For centuries, there was a zero sum game in which some people became substantially richer at the same time that others became substantially poorer. This insight has been further developed by contemporary scholarship on "racialized capitalism," which emphasizes the intertwining of racial subordination and economic progress in U.S. history.[8]

However, in some versions of world-systems theory, it is assumed that this zero sum process continues down to the present moment. So logically if working-class people in Scandinavia used trade unions and social democratic parties to win a significantly higher standard of living, this can only mean that they have pushed people in Africa or Latin America into greater poverty. To put it bluntly, the achievements of advanced welfare states in Scandinavia depend on the continuation of imperial exploitation elsewhere in the world. This argument is a contemporary version of Lenin's claim that the fruits of imperialism created a "labor aristocracy" in developed countries whose interests diverged radically from those of the rest of the working class.

Lenin's argument was already highly problematic in 1917, and its contemporary version has no empirical foundation. The reality is that improvements in living standards in Scandinavia are the result of sophisticated technologies that have driven down the price of key goods and services. There is no longer a mechanism through which improvements for some necessarily come at the expense of others. To be sure, the smart phones that are ubiquitous in Scandinavia depend on tantalum, which comes from conflict zones in the Democratic Republic of the Congo. But this is a contingent connection, not a necessary one. If the Congo had an effective government, the rest of the world would likely pay a higher price for the needed minerals. Before OPEC, developed nations were able to get petroleum at bargain basement prices, but once the cartel was formed, those same developed nations were able and willing to pay a price that transferred considerable wealth to the oil-producing nations.

Moreover, the fact that a billion people in India and China moved into the global middle class over the last two decades suggests that the world economy is not locked into some fixed ratio between those who are rich and those who are poor. Even with private profit making, it has been possible to shrink the share of the world's population that lives in poverty. So there is reason to believe that with reforms designed to generate economic progress in the least-developed nations, substantial further progress could be made.

The main difficulty with world-systems theory is that it fails to recognize that the specific global rules and institutions in place at a particular time do not flow from the logic of global capitalism; they are the result of particular political settlements depending upon the relative strength of different nations and different interests. Moreover, those rules and institutions keep changing, and they will continue to change, as I argue in chapter 6. The Bretton Woods regime that ended in 1973 had many weaknesses, but it did make possible significant economic and social reforms in the developed market economies. The same cannot be said for the more market-oriented global regime that has existed since the early 1980s; it has reinforced pressures for austerity and the reversal of earlier reforms. The point is that this global regime has failed, and it could be replaced with something better if there were enough political pressure.

When these constraining rules and institutions are labeled as the machinery of global capitalism, the consequence is to reinforce arguments made by the defenders of the status quo, who insist that there is no way to organize the world economy other than around free trade, free movement of capital, and extensive protections for investors. The reality is that global commerce could flourish under a wide variety of different rules governing trade, finance, and intellectual property, and it is not difficult to imagine changes in these rules that would make it substantially easier to wage struggles in both nations and global regions for greater equality, stronger democracy, and more environmental protection.

FUTILITY: THE LIMITS TO REFORM

In *Rhetorics of Reaction,* Albert Hirschman draws our attention to the kinds of arguments used to oppose economic and social reforms from the French Revolution onward. He identifies three core claims—jeopardy, perversity, and futility. Jeopardy is the kind of argument that Hayek made in *The Road to Serfdom*—providing people with more protections from the market will inevitably create all-powerful states that will destroy privacy and individual liberty. Perversity is the claim that reforms will hurt the very people they are intended to help, as in Malthus's claim that England's generous Poor Law created the poverty that it was intended to alleviate. But the most important claim has always been futility—that a given reform simply cannot work given the nature and structure of the existing social order, which means that instituting the reform will inevitably produce chaos and disorder. As Hirschman shows, such reactionary futility arguments have been mobilized against a whole series of measures that are now taken-for-granted features of modernity.

The complication is that Marx and Engels developed their own version of the futility thesis in arguing that the only way to overcome the evils of capitalism was through socialist revolution.[9] They insisted that reformist strategies were an exercise in futility because the logic of capital accumulation would inevitably reassert itself, so that even if reforms were won, they would ultimately be reversed. If, for example, workers were able to win major wage gains, the capitalists would find a way to drive wages back down. If the capitalists found that parliaments elected through universal suffrage were interfering with their profits, they would simply opt for dictatorship.

This Marxist futility thesis continues to have influence because the power of the ownership class has been able to block policies that have considerable public and legislative support. This has led some to believe that there is a fundamental tension between real democracy and private ownership, since control over investment decisions gives the investor class disproportionate political power.[10] But it is possible to recognize the reality of this "structural power of capital" while also seeing limitations on that power.

One factor that weakens this structural power is the difficulty that owners have in maintaining a unified position against continuous and ongoing pressures from civil society. We have seen this with climate change. For a long time, other businesses stood with the fossil fuel industry in denying the existence of a problem. But over time, huge cracks emerged in the ownership class that opened the way for most governments to pursue more aggressive policies to reduce dependence on fossil fuels.

The possibility of these opinion shifts helps make sense of the considerable variation across developed market societies in their institutional arrangements. The argument that it is futile to attempt to reform a system of private ownership to achieve major reductions in poverty, racism, gender bias, or exploitative foreign relations runs up against the reality of considerable variation across the developed market societies. Given these substantial variations, how can one claim that capitalism is inherently incompatible with any specific reform?

To be sure, we know all too well that reforms that are won at one historical moment can be reversed later on. The right-wing project in the United States has focused for decades on undoing the reforms of Franklin Roosevelt's New Deal.[11] The right has won some of those battles, such as achieving significant reductions in the share of the labor force represented by labor unions, with devastating consequences for employment security and income inequality. But the right has lost other battles. Despite decades of trying, they have not yet been able to "reform" Social Security to end the protections that it provides to the elderly. The point, however, is that which of these battles is won or lost is not a consequence of the logic of an economic system; it depends on which side is more successful in mobilizing people and dollars to shape political outcomes.

The larger point is that both right- and left-wing versions of the futility argument rely on a problematic foundation of economic determinism. The claim is that reforms that are incompatible with the basic structure of a profit-oriented economy will inevitably be defeated in much the same way that the immune system of the body mobilizes against unwanted intruders. However, this way of thinking has been repeatedly disproved through historical experience. Partisans on the right and on the left argued that such key reforms as the federal income tax, the forty-hour work week, and collective bargaining, which recognized the right to strike, were inherently incompatible with a free market or capitalist economy. And yet such reforms have been won and maintained in many places.

The left-wing version of the futility thesis also poses a problem for reform efforts. During the heroic epoch of the working-class movement in Europe and North America from roughly 1848 to 1968, there was often an effective synergy between those who were fighting for reforms and those who believed that the purpose of the reform struggles was to teach workers the necessity of challenging and transcending capitalism. Left-wing militants who embraced the futility thesis often brought to the movement valuable strategic ideas and an orientation to building effective organizations that were indispensable to winning critical reforms.

Today, however, that industrial working class is an ever-shrinking portion of the labor force, and building reform coalitions is an inherently more complex task that requires bringing together a far more heterogeneous alliance of constituencies. The fundamental challenge in assembling such coalitions is persuading participants of the possibility of winning real victories. In this context, contemporary versions of the futility thesis can be counterproductive. So, for example, when the project is assembling a powerful coalition to win government action to shift away from fossil fuels to avert catastrophic climate change, the voices who insist that such a reform cannot possibly be won as long as capitalism exists might well demobilize potential supporters.

My view is that there are great advantages for the left in replacing the futility thesis with the political equivalent of agnosticism. This means starting with a frank acknowledgment that we cannot know in advance what reforms may or may not be winnable without a radical transformation of the economic system. This agnosticism also recognizes that the barriers to any significant reform will be formidable. One has to overcome the considerable class power exercised by those who hold a disproportionate share of society's wealth and also change the global rules and institutions that enhance that class power. On top of this, there is the challenge of maintaining sufficient unity within a heterogeneous reform coalition to wage a sustained battle against the power of the wealthy.

However, this kind of healthy agnosticism could be precisely what is needed to create the broad democratic movements necessary to address the economic, political, and environmental challenges we face. Karl Polanyi ended *The Great Transformation* with the words of the nineteenth-century socialist thinker Robert Owen: "Should any causes of evil be irremovable by the new powers which men are about to acquire, they will know that they are necessary and unavoidable evils; and childish, unavailing complaints will cease to be made."[12] If we interpret Owen as using "men" to connote both men and women and "new powers" as a reference to both democratic governance and technological capabilities, he is suggesting that being agnostic about what kinds of reform are ultimately possible can empower us to wage concerted, sustained, and realistic reform struggles. Polanyi rephrases this agnosticism by insisting that resignation to the realities of human existence can provide human beings with "indomitable courage and strength" to make necessary reforms.[13]

Polanyi is an exemplary guide here because he is so clear in delineating the goal of this reform project. It is not something abstract, such as human emancipation or the end of alienation. It is, rather, expanding and deepening democracy so that markets are ultimately subordinated to democratic politics. For centuries, people have struggled to establish democratic practices and a structure of legal rights to overcome the power of monarchs, dictators, and aspiring autocrats. As we know from recent experiences, this is an unceasing battle that is never won definitively. Polanyi's point is that success in extending democracy to the economic realm is absolutely central if self-government is to be preserved and strengthened.

This insight is particularly relevant at this historical moment, when we are witness to a global retreat from democracy as a growing number of elected leaders trample on democratic norms in a rush to consolidate their personal power. In virtually every case, these leaders mobilize ethnic or religious divisions and intensify regional or global disputes as a means to weaken or silence their domestic opponents. As in the 1920s and 1930s, the revival of authoritarian nationalism is a morbid symptom of the dysfunctions of the global economy. Unable to protect themselves from growing economic uncertainty and instability, many voters choose to support one or another divisive leader who promises to make that particular nation "great again."

The threat that this flight from democracy will prove contagious cannot be exaggerated. With more leaders embracing extreme nationalism, the capacity for global cooperation to meet challenges such as economic crises, climate crises, and refugee crises diminishes and the threat of open conflict increases.

We saw as recently as 2008–2009 that only a very high level of cooperative global crisis management prevented the economic downturn from becoming a global depression. Faced with another similar crisis, such cooperation might not materialize. Moreover, the extreme weather events that can be expected as a consequence of global climate change might also intensify international divisions and corrode global cooperation. More nations are likely to turn to leaders who embrace extreme nationalism and "illiberal democracy"as the world becomes an ever more dangerous and uncertain place.

The most promising way to avoid this dangerous downward spiral is to reform the global economy and national economies to protect people from high levels of economic uncertainty and mounting environmental threats. Most of the policies needed to do this are already known, but one key obstacle is the illusion that capitalism is an unchanging and unchangeable system whose inner logic must be obeyed. If we can shatter that illusion, then we have a far better chance to create majoritarian reform coalitions strong enough to overcome the opposition of those who are wedded to the present unjust distribution of economic rewards. Success is far from certain, but the alternative is unthinkable.

Notes

1. THE CAPITALIST ILLUSION

1. Freud argued that illusions are different from errors in that they are connected to wishes. Freud, *Future*, p. 39. The wish that is associated with the illusion of capitalism is that society be governed by a system that is coherent and predictable rather than the capricious choices of political leaders. Whether one is a supporter or a critic of the existing order, one's views could well be shaped by this wish.

2. Judis, *Populist Explosion*.

3. Katznelson, *Fear Itself*.

4. Esping-Andersen, *Three Worlds of Welfare Capitalism*.

5. The U.S. Chamber of Commerce, for example, favors increased infrastructure spending. See www.uschamber.com/infrastructure?tab = position#timeline.

6. Mayer, *Dark Money*; Skocpol and Hertel-Fernandez, "Koch Network."

7. Krippner, *Capitalizing on Crisis*, chap. 2.

8. The concept of cognitive capture is used by Willem H. Buitler to explain the failures of Federal Reserve policy leading up to the 2008 crisis. "Central Banks and Financial Crises." The term means that regulators have adopted the worldview of those that they regulate.

9. The account of the 1930s that has shaped my thinking is Polanyi, *Great Transformation*.

10. Some recent examples are Nee and Swedberg, *On Capitalism*; Hodgson, *Conceptualizing Capitalism*.

11. It would be more accurate to call it an "asocial theory" because it largely ignores society and social institutions. However, earlier social theories such as late nineteenth-century social Darwinism had similar characteristics.

12. Beard, *Economic Interpretation*.

13. Riesman, Glazer, and Denney, *Lonely Crowd*; Mills, *Power Elite*; Bell, *Coming of Post-Industrial Society*.

14. For data showing declining sales of books by sociologists after the 1970s, see Gans, "Best-Sellers."

15. See Blyth, *Austerity*.

16. Key works include Crouch and Streeck, *Political Economy of Modern Capitalism*, and Hall and Soskice, *Varieties of Capitalism*. For fuller references, see Block, "Varieties of What?"

17. William Jordan, "Democrats More Divided on Socialism," YouGov, January 28, 2016, https://today.yougov.com/news/2016/01/28/democrats-remain-divided-socialism/.

18. Carroll, *Annotated Alice*, pp. 268–269.

19. www.sdsrebels.com/index.htm, accessed December 15, 2016.

20. Full disclosure: I was also one of those New Left Marxists who helped to reintroduce the concept of capitalism into academic debates. Block, *Revising State Theory*.

21. Wallerstein, *Modern World-System*; Edwards, Reich, and Weisskopf, *Capitalist System*.

22. M. Friedman, *Capitalism and Freedom*; Rand, *Capitalism*.

23. Brick, *Transcending Capitalism*, p. 309.

24. Kristol, *Two Cheers for Capitalism*.

25. Gilder, *Wealth and Poverty*.

26. McArthur, "Great Depression."

27. Block, "Deconstructing Capitalism."

28. On Friedman and his colleagues at Chicago and in the Mont Pelerin Society, see Mirowski and Plehwe, *Road from Mont Pelerin*; Burgin, *Great Persuasion*; Jones, *Masters of the Universe*.

29. Krippner, *Capitalizing on Crisis.*

30. One important strand of popularization linked this vision of capitalism to Christianity. See Moreton, *To Serve God and Wal-Mart.*

31. On Polanyi, see Block and Somers, *Power of Market Fundamentalism.* On Hirschman, see Adelman, *Worldly Philosopher.* See also Gibson-Graham, *End of Capitalism.*

32. On Hale, see Fried, *Progressive Assault on Laissez-Faire.* See also D. Kennedy, *Sexy Dressing* and *Critique of Adjudication;* Klare, "Workplace Democracy" and "Critical Perspectives"; Unger, *False Necessity.*

33. Evans, "Is an Alternative Globalization Possible?"; Krippner, *Capitalizing on Crisis;* Somers, *Genealogies of Citizenship;* Zelizer, *Purchase of Intimacy.*

34. Bell, *Coming of Post-Industrial Society;* Hirschhorn, *Beyond Mechanization;* Sklar, *United States as a Developing Country.* See also Brick, *Transcending Capitalism.*

2. ELABORATING AN ALTERNATIVE

1. This argument was developed initially by legal realists prior to the New Deal and more recently by "critical realists." See the section entitled "Critical Legal Realism in a Nutshell" in Davis and Klare, "Transformative Constitutionalism"; see also Fried, *Progressive Assault.*

2. One recent example is the theory of "relational contract," which gives rise to legally enforceable obligations of good faith. See Speidel, "'Duty' of Good Faith."

3. Desmond, *Evicted.*

4. Lichtenstein, *Labor's War at Home,* chap. 7.

5. Block and Somers, *Power of Market Fundamentalism,* chap. 6.

6. Bell, "Models and Realities."

7. Skocpol and Williamson, *Tea Party.*

8. Eichengreen, *Hall of Mirrors,* pp. 210–11.

9. Alan Greenspan cited in Andrews, "Greenspan Concedes Error."

10. Gamble, *Hayek,* p . 38.

11. Block and Somers, *Power of Market Fundamentalism*, chap. 3.

12. Shock therapy is a strategy for moving rapidly to a market economy by quickly privatizing assets and shrinking the state's role in the economy. The definitive critique is Klein, *Shock Doctrine*.

13. Woodruff, *Money Unmade;* Reddaway and Glinski, *Tragedy of Russia's Reforms;* Volkov, "Between Economy and the State."

14. A contrasting view was presented by Stiglitz, *Whither Socialism?*

15. Polanyi, *Great Transformation;* Block and Somers, *Power of Market Fundamentalism.*

16. Block, "Contradictory Logics of Financialization."

17. A patent, for example, gives the owner the exclusive right to incorporate a particular technology into a firm's products. If, for example, the patent is for a pharmaceutical to treat a particular medical condition, the government has eliminated competition to sell that product for the duration of the patent. Jessop, "Knowledge as a Fictitious Commodity."

18. See Benkler, *Wealth of Networks.*

19. For a particularly explicit argument along these lines, see T. Friedman, *Lexus and the Olive Tree.*

20. Kenny, "Why Factory Jobs Are Shrinking Everywhere."

21. Knight, "China Is Building a Robot Army of Model Workers."

22. Block, *Postindustrial Possibilities.*

23. Polanyi analyzes this as a conflict between habitation and improvement. *Great Transformation*, chap. 3.

24. Data are from the U.S. Bureau of Labor Statistics, "Employment by Major Industry Sector," www.bls.gov/emp/ep_table_201 .htm.

25. See Block and Keller, *State of Innovation.*

26. Kirkpatrick and Smith, "Infrastructural Limits to Growth."

27. Baiocchi, *Militants and Citizens;* Baiocchi and Ganuza, *Popular Democracy.*

28. Estimate from American Society of Civil Engineers, "2017: Infrastructure Report Card," 2017, www.infrastructurereportcard.org /the-impact/economic-impact/.

29. One key example is developed in Lew Daly, "What Is Our Public GDP?" Demos, 2014, www.demos.org/publication/what-our-public-gdp-valuing-government-twenty-first-century-economy.

30. Stiglitz, Sen, and Fitoussi, *Mis-measuring Our Lives.*

3. THE ILLUSION THAT DEMOCRACY THREATENS THE ECONOMY

1. Madison, *Federalist Papers*, no. 10.

2. This continuity is the theme of MacLean, *Democracy in Chains.*

3. See, for example, Buchanan, *Politics of Public Choice.*

4. For a recent review of the complexities of these investor dispute mechanisms, see United Nations Conference on Trade and Development, *World Investment Report 2015.*

5. I recognize, however, that the class power of the wealthy constrains and limits the effectiveness of democratic institutions. This issue is addressed in chapter 5 and in the afterword. The argument here is that stronger democratic institutions improve the ability of an economy to meet human needs.

6. Winters, *Oligarchy*, especially chap. 5.

7. The figure is from Opensecrets.org, but other research shows that an equal number of shadow lobbyists do similar work but avoid the registration requirement. Tim LaPira, "How Much Lobbying Is There in Washington? It's DOUBLE What You Think," November 25, 2013, http://sunlightfoundation.com/2013/11/25/how-much-lobbying-is-there-in-washington-its-double-what-you-think/.

8. Tocqueville, *Democracy in America.*

9. Robertson, *Temple of Invention.*

10. Tocqueville, *Democracy in America*, vol. 2, p. 311.

11. Christopers, *Great Leveler.*

12. Piven, *Challenging Authority*, ch. 4.

13. Wright, *Sharing the Prize.*

14. Matthijs, "The Euro's 'Winner-Take-All' Political Economy."

15. Nelson and Stephens, "Do Social Investment Policies Produce More and Better Jobs?"

16. Goldin and Katz, *Race*, chap. 9.

17. For a prescient diagnosis, see Crouch, *Post-Democracy*.

18. Piketty, *Capital in the Twenty-First Century*.

19. D. Baker, *Rigged*; Christophers, *Great Leveler*.

4. THE ILLUSION THAT GREED IS GOOD

1. M. Friedman, "Social Responsibility."

2. Block, *Postindustrial Possibilities*, chap. 3.

3. M. Friedman and R. Friedman, *Free to Choose*, p. 57.

4. Smith, *Theory of Moral Sentiments*, p. 173.

5. Ibid., pp. 97–98.

6. Smith, *Wealth of Nations*, p. 144.

7. Durkheim, *Division of Labor in Society*, p. 160.

8. Swedberg, *Max Weber Dictionary*, pp. 3–4, 25–27.

9. Weber, *Protestant Ethic and the Spirit of Capitalism*.

10. Bell, *Cultural Contradictions of Capitalism*.

11. Zelizer, *Purchase of Intimacy*, and "How I Became a Relational Economic Sociologist."

12. Draper, "Toxic Pharmacist."

13. Burns, *Goddess*.

14. For more of these examples, see Soltes, *Why They Do It*.

15. Brooks, *Bobos in Paradise*.

16. TyreeHageman, "From Silicon Valley to Wall Street."

17. On the difficulties of prosecuting corporate criminals, see Garrett, *Too Big to Jail*. Eisinger, *Chickenshit Club*, emphasizes the disincentives for federal prosecutors to take on cases against powerful corporate entities.

18. Fried, *Progressive Assault*.

19. Teles, *Rise of the Conservative Legal Movement*.

20. McLean and Nocera, *All the Devils Are Here*.

21. Useem, *Executive Defense*.

22. The most eloquent critic of this practice has been William Lazonick, *Sustainable Prosperity* and "Profits without Prosperity."

23. This maxim was widely used at the time of the transition of post-Soviet societies. This was part of the justification for shock therapy;

putting the property rights in the hands of private owners took priority over everything else.

24. This is the perversity thesis analyzed by Hirschman, *Rhetoric of Reaction,* and discussed by Block and Somers, *Power of Market Fundamentalism,* chap. 6.

25. For evidence and argument on the sovereignty of the individual in American culture, see W. Baker, *America's Crisis of Values.*

26. Page and Jacobs, *Class War?;* Norton and Ariely, "Building a Better America."

5. THE ILLUSION OF AN UNCHANGING SYSTEM

1. The sixteenth-century argument is made by Wallerstein, *Modern World-System;* the later argument is made by Wood, *Origin of Capitalism.*

2. Sahlins, *Culture and Practical Reason.*

3. M. Friedman and Friedman, *Free to Choose,* chap. 8.

4. Freeman and Medoff, *What Do Unions Do?*

5. Block, *Postindustrial Possibilities,* chap. 4.

6. The use of such compensation schemes is described in Blasi, Freeman, and Kruse, *Citizen's Wage,* chap 3.

7. Smith, *Wealth of Nations,* p. 91.

8. Ibid.

9. Ferguson and Rogers, *Right Turn.*

10. Block and Somers, *Power of Market Fundamentalism,* chap. 7.

11. Goldin and Katz, *Race,* chap. 9.

12. *Historical Statistics of the United States, Millennial Edition,* Table Ba 652–669, Table 1018–1022, and U.S. Bureau of Labor Statistics, "Employment by Major Industry Sector," https://data.bls.gov/cgi-bin/print.pl /emp/ep_table_201.htm. Note that the 2004 farming data includes fishing and forestry employment.

13. Sklar, *United States as a Developing Country,* chap. 5.

14. Newfield, *Unmaking the Public University.*

15. Eaton et al., "Financialization of U.S. Higher Education."

16. Wolfgang Streeck has argued that the institutional arrangements I am describing have been in rapid decline in recent years. See

Re-Forming Capitalism and his response to me in chapter 10 of *How Will Capitalism End?* I would argue, however, that Streeck has exaggerated this decline and that many of the cooperative arrangements that have sustained German manufacturing remain in place.

17. These arguments are developed in Morel, Palier, and Palme, *Towards a Social Investment Welfare State?*

18. This argument about the productive role of consumers is developed by Alic, "Everyone an Innovator."

19. Anti-union campaigns triggered concern that the U.S. was no longer in compliance with international human rights standards. See Compa, *Unfair Advantage.*

20. This was as of 2012 as reported by Eurostat, "Manufacturing Statistics—NACE 2," August 2016, figure 2.

21. Pontusson, *Inequality and Prosperity*, chap. 3.

22. Berger, *Making in America.*

23. Kwon, "Politics of Globalization and National Economy."

24. Thelen, *How Institutions Evolve.*

25. Brynjolfsson and McAfee, *Second Machine Age.*

26. Lopez, "Culture Change Management in Long-Term Care."

27. Piketty, *Capital in the Twenty-First Century*, pp. 340, 348.

28. https://taxfoundation.org/article/us-federal-individual-income-tax-rates-history-1913–2013-nominal-and-inflation-adjusted-brackets/.

29. Block, *Revising State Theory*, chap. 3.

6. THE ILLUSION OF GLOBAL ORDER ORGANIZED BY CAPITALISM

1. T. Friedman, *Lexus and the Olive Tree*, p. 195.

2. The history of this idea is discussed in Hirschman, *The Passions and the Interests.*

3. Block, *Revising State Theory*, chap. 3.

4. Block, "Controlling Global Finance."

5. This was the period of "embedded liberalism." Ruggie, "International Regimes."

6. I criticized this way of thinking in *Vampire State*, pp. 185–275.

7. For a listing, see Global Policy Forum at https://www.globalpolicy.org/us-westward-expansion/26024.html.

8. See, for example, Mann, *Sources of Social Power.*

9. For a critique of the hypocrisy of free trade advocates in the U.S. and the U.K., see Chang, *Kicking Away the Ladder.*

10. Beckert, *Empire of Cotton.*

11. Weiss and Thurbon, "Business of Buying American."

12. Krippner, *Capitalizing on Crisis*, chap. 4.

13. P. Kennedy, *Rise and Fall.*

14. There is a vast literature on global institutions and global regimes. On the international monetary system, see Eichengreen, *Globalizing Capital.* On the proliferation of global regulatory schemes, see Braithwaite, *Regulatory Capitalism.*

15. Keck and Sikkink, *Activists beyond Borders;* Appelbaum and Lichtenstein, *Achieving Workers' Rights.*

16. Polanyi, *Great Transformation*, chap. 2.

17. This dilemma is elaborated in Berman, *Primacy of Politics.*

18. For similar accounts, see Eichengreen, *Hall of Mirrors*, and Varoufakis, *And the Weak Suffer What They Must?*

19. See the powerful critique of the euro in Streeck, *Buying Time*, chap. 3.

20. Blyth, *Austerity.*

21. Block, "A Neo-Polanyian Theory of Economic Crises."

22. Skidelsky, *John Maynard Keynes.*

23. Eatwell and Taylor, *Global Finance at Risk.*

24. Bivens and Blair, "A Financial Transaction Tax."

25. For a similar strategic perspective, see Sandbrook, *Reinventing the Left in the Global South.*

7. BEYOND ILLUSIONS

1. Block and Somers, *Power of Market Fundamentalism*, chap. 6.

2. Foster, *Productivity and Prosperity.*

3. Block, *Postindustrial Possibilities*, chap. 7.

4. Table 2.5, Transportation Sector Energy Consumption, U.S. Energy Information Administration, www.eia.gov/totalenergy/data /monthly/pdf/sec2_11.pdf.

5. Prasad, *Land of Too Much*, p. 46.

6. Bernanke, "Global Saving Glut."

7. The estimate is from the 2017 report card from the American Society of Civil Engineers, www.infrastructurereportcard.org/.

8. In the post-2008 period of historically low interest rates, corporations around the world have dramatically increased their issuance of bonds, with total issues reaching an astonishing $3.6 trillion level in 2016. Platt, "Corporates Lead Surge." It seems highly likely that some significant portion of this debt will turn bad when over-leveraged firms are unable to keep up interest payments.

9. Hockett and Omarova, "Finance Franchise."

10. Parijs and Vanderborght, *Basic Income.*

11. Many of these ideas are addressed in Stiglitz, *Rewriting the Rules.*

AFTERWORD

1. On the new liberals, see Freeden, *New Liberalism;* Kloppenberg, *Uncertain Victory;* Rodgers, *Atlantic Crossings.*

2. The "varieties of capitalism" terminology continues to be used, but as an intellectual movement, it had lost momentum even before the global financial crisis. Important early contributions were Hollingsworth and Boyer, *Contemporary Capitalism;* Crouch and Streeck, *Political Economy of Modern Capitalism.*

3. Another important precursor was Zysman, *Governments, Markets, and Growth.*

4. For useful reviews and critiques of this literature, see Coates, *Varieties.*

5. To be sure, the widely cited introduction to Hall and Soskice's *Varieties of Capitalism* asserted a sharp dichotomy between liberal market economies (LMEs) and coordinated market economies (CMEs) based on the relationship between business firms and government. However, history and subsequent scholarship have not been kind to this binary.

6. Peck and Theodore, "Variegated Capitalism"; Jessop, "What Follows Neo-Liberalism?"

7. Wallerstein, *Modern World-System* and *Essential Wallerstein.*

8. Dawson, "Hidden in Plain Sight."

9. Block, "Deconstructing Capitalism."

10. Lindblom, *Politics and Markets,* chap. 3; Block, *Revising State Theory.*

11. Phillips-Fein, *Invisible Hands.*

12. Polanyi, *Great Transformation,* p. 268.

13. Ibid., p. 268. Part of Polanyi's agenda here is to discourage the political hubris that flows from a utopian exaggeration of human perfectibility. See Block, "Karl Polanyi and Human Freedom."

Bibliography

Adelman, Jeremy. *Worldly Philosopher: The Odyssey of Albert O. Hirschman.* Princeton: Princeton University Press, 2013.

Alic, John. "Everyone an Innovator." Pp. 236–260 in Fred Block and Matthew R. Keller, eds., *State of Innovation.* Boulder: Paradigm, 2011.

Andrews, Edmund. "Greenspan Concedes Error on Regulation." *New York Times,* October 24, 2008.

Appelbaum, Richard P., and Nelson Lichtenstein, eds. *Achieving Workers' Rights in the Global Economy.* Ithaca: Cornell University Press, 2016.

Baiocchi, Gianpaolo. *Militants and Citizens: The Politics of Participatory Democracy in Porto Alegre.* Stanford: Stanford University Press, 2005.

Baiocchi, Gianpaolo, and Ernesto Ganuza. *Popular Democracy and the Paradox of Participation.* Stanford: Stanford University Press, 2017.

Baker, Dean. *Rigged: How Globalization and the Rules of the Modern Economy Were Structured to Make the Rich Richer.* Washington, D.C.: Center for Economic Policy Research, 2016.

Baker, Wayne. *America's Crisis of Values: Reality and Perception.* Princeton: Princeton University Press, 2005.

Beard, Charles. *An Economic Interpretation of the Constitution of the United States.* New York: Free Press, 1935 [1913].

Beckert, Sven. *Empire of Cotton: A Global History.* New York: Knopf, 2014.

Bell, Daniel. *The Coming of Post-Industrial Society: A Venture in Social Forecasting.* New York: Basic Books, 1973.

———. *The Cultural Contradictions of Capitalism.* New York: Basic Books, 1976.

———. "Models and Reality in Economic Discourse." Pp. 46–80 in Daniel Bell and Irving Kristol, eds., *The Crisis in Economic Theory.* New York: Basic Books, 1981.

Benkler, Yochai. *The Wealth of Networks: How Social Production Transforms Markets and Freedom.* New Haven: Yale University Press, 2006.

Berger, Suzanne. *Making in America: From Innovation to Market.* Cambridge: MIT Press, 2013.

Berman, Sheri. *The Primacy of Politics: Social Democracy and the Making of Europe's Twentieth Century.* New York: Cambridge University Press, 2006.

Bernanke, Ben. "The Global Saving Glut and the U.S. Current Account Deficit." Speech. March 10, 2005, Federal Reserve Board. www.federalreserve.gov/boarddocs/speeches/2005/200503102/.

Bivens, Josh, and Hunter Blair. "A Financial Transaction Tax Would Help Ensure Wall Street Works for Main Street." Economic Policy Institute, July 28, 2016. www.epi.org/publication/a-financial-transaction-tax-would-help-ensure-wall-street-works-for-main-street/.

Blasi, Joseph R., Richard Freeman, and Douglas Kruse. *The Citizen's Share: Reducing Inequality in the 21st Century.* New Haven: Yale University Press, 2014.

Block, Fred L. "The Contradictory Logics of Financialization: Bringing Together Hyman Minsky and Karl Polanyi." *Politics & Society* 44:1 (2016) 3–13.

———. "Controlling Global Finance." *World Policy Journal* 13:3 (1996): 24–34.

———. "Deconstructing Capitalism as a System." *Rethinking Marxism* 12:3 (2000): 83–97.

———. "Karl Polanyi and Human Freedom." Pp. 165–181 in Michael Brie and Claus Thomasberger, eds., *Karl Polanyi's Vision of a Socialist Transformation.* Montreal: Black Rose, 2018.

———. "A Neo-Polanyian Theory of Economic Crises." *American Journal of Economics and Sociology* 74:2 (2015): 361–378.

————. *The Origins of International Economic Disorder.* Berkeley: University of California Press, 1977.

————. *Postindustrial Possibilities: A Critique of Economic Discourse.* Berkeley: University of California Press, 1990.

————. *Revising State Theory: Essays in Politics and Postindustrialism.* Philadelphia: Temple, 1987.

————. *The Vampire State and Other Myths and Fallacies about the U.S. Economy.* New York: New Press, 1996.

————. "Varieties of What? Should We Still be Using the Concept of Capitalism?" *Political Power and Social Theory* 23 (2012): 271–293.

Block, Fred, and Matthew R. Keller, eds. *State of Innovation: The U.S. Government's Role in Technology Development.* Boulder: Paradigm, 2011.

Block, Fred, and Margaret R. Somers. *The Power of Market Fundamentalism: Karl Polanyi's Critique.* Cambridge: Harvard University Press, 2014.

Blyth, Mark. *Austerity: The History of a Dangerous Idea.* New York: Oxford University Press, 2013.

Braithwaite, John. *Regulatory Capitalism: How It Works, Ideas for Making It Better.* Cheltenham, U.K.: Edward Elgar, 2008.

Brick, Howard. *Transcending Capitalism: Visions of a New Society in Modern American Thought.* Ithaca: Cornell University Press, 2006.

Brooks, David. *Bobos in Paradise: The New Upper Class and How They Got There.* New York: Simon and Schuster, 2000.

Brynjolfsson, Erik, and Andrew McAfee. *The Second Machine Age.* New York: Norton, 2014.

Buchanan, James. *The Politics of Public Choice.* Indianapolis: Liberty Fund, 2000.

Buitler, Willem H. "Central Banks and Financial Crises." Discussion Paper no. 619. Financial Markets Group, London School of Economics, 2008.

Burgin, Angus. *The Great Persuasion: Reinventing Free Markets since the Depression.* Cambridge: Harvard University Press, 2012.

Burns, Jennifer. *Goddess of the Market: Ayn Rand and the American Right.* New York: Oxford University Press, 2009.

Carroll, Lewis. *The Annotated Alice: Alice's Adventures in Wonderland and Through the Looking Glass.* New York: Bramhall, 1960.

Chang, Ha-Joon. *Kicking Away the Ladder: Development Strategy in Historical Perspective.* London: Anthem, 2002.

Christophers, Brett. *The Great Leveler: Capitalism and Competition in the Court of Law.* Cambridge: Harvard University Press, 2016.

Coates, David, ed. *Varieties of Capitalism, Varieties of Approaches.* Basingstoke, U.K.: Palgrave, 2005.

Compa, Lance. *Unfair Advantage: Workers' Freedom of Association in the United States under International Human Rights Standards.* Ithaca: Cornell University Press, 2000.

Crouch, Colin. *Post-Democracy.* Oxford: Polity Press, 2004.

Crouch, Colin, and Wolfgang Streeck, eds. *Political Economy of Modern Capitalism.* Thousand Oaks, Calif.: Sage, 1997.

Davis, Dennis M., and Karl Klare. "Transformative Constitutionalism and the Common and Customary Law." *South African Journal on Human Rights* 26:3 (2010): 403–509.

Dawson, Michael. "Hidden in Plain Sight: A Note on Legitimation Crises and the Racial Order." *Critical Historical Studies* (Spring 2016): 143–161.

Desmond, Matthew. *Evicted: Poverty and Profit in an American City.* New York: Crown, 2016.

Draper, Robert. "The Toxic Pharmacist." *New York Times Magazine,* June 8, 2003.

Durkheim, Émile. *The Division of Labor in Society.* Trans. W.D. Halls. New York: Free Press, 1984 [1893].

Eaton, Charlie, et al. "The Financialization of U.S. Higher Education." *Socio-Economic Review* 14:3 (2016): 507–535.

Eatwell, John, and Lance Taylor. *Global Finance at Risk: The Case for International Regulation.* New York: New Press, 2000.

Edwards, Richard, Michael Reich, and Thomas Weisskopf. *The Capitalist System: A Radical Analysis of American Society.* Englewood Cliffs, N.J.: Prentice Hall, 1972.

Eichengreen, Barry. *Globalizing Capital: A History of the International Monetary System.* Princeton: Princeton University Press, 1996.

———. *Hall of Mirrors: The Great Depression, the Great Recession, and the Uses—and Misuses—of History.* New York: Oxford University Press, 2015.

Eisinger, Jesse. *The Chickenshit Club.* New York: Simon and Schuster, 2017.

Esping-Andersen, Gosta. *The Three Worlds of Welfare Capitalism.* Princeton: Princeton University Press, 1990.

Evans, Peter. "Is an Alternative Globalization Possible?" *Politics & Society* 36:2 (2008): 271–305.

Ferguson, Thomas, and Joel Rogers. *Right Turn: The Decline of the Democrats and the Future of American Politics.* New York: Hill and Wang, 1987.

Foster, Karen R. *Productivity and Prosperity: A Historical Sociology of Productivist Thought.* Toronto: University of Toronto Press, 2016.

Freeden, Michael. *The New Liberalism: An Ideology of Social Reform.* Oxford: Clarendon Press, 1978.

Freeman, Richard, and James Medoff. *What Do Unions Do?* New York: Basic Books, 1984.

Freud, Sigmund. *The Future of an Illusion.* Trans. James Strachey. New York: Norton, 1989 [1927].

Fried, Barbara H. *The Progressive Assault on Laissez-Faire: Robert Hale and the First Law and Economics Movement.* Cambridge: Harvard University Press, 2001.

Friedman, Milton. *Capitalism and Freedom.* Chicago: University of Chicago Press, 1962.

———. "The Social Responsibility of Business Is to Increase Its Profits." *New York Times Magazine*, September 13, 1970.

Friedman, Milton, and Rose Friedman. *Free to Choose.* New York: Harcourt Brace Jovanovich, 1980.

Friedman, Thomas. *The Lexus and the Olive Tree.* New York: Farrar Straus and Giroux, 1999.

Gamble, Andrew. *Hayek: The Iron Cage of Liberty.* Boulder: Westview, 1996.

Gans, Herbert. "Best-Sellers by Sociologists: An Exploratory Study." *Contemporary Sociology* 26 (March 1997): 131–135.

Garrett, Brandon L. *Too Big to Jail: How Prosecutors Compromise with Corporations.* Cambridge: Belknap, 2014.

Gibson-Graham, J.K. *The End of Capitalism [as we knew it]: A Feminist Critique of Political Economy.* Cambridge, Mass.: Blackwell, 1996.

Gilder, George. *Wealth and Poverty.* New York: Basic Books, 1981.

Goldin, Claudia, and Lawrence F. Katz. *The Race between Education and Technology.* Cambridge: Belknap, 2008.

Gordon, Robert J. *The Rise and Fall of American Growth.* Princeton: Princeton University Press, 2016.

Hall, Peter, and David Soskice, eds. *Varieties of Capitalism.* New York: Oxford University Press, 2001.

Hayek, Friedrich. *The Road to Serfdom*. Chicago: University of Chicago Press, 1944.

Hirschhorn, Larry. *Beyond Mechanization: Work and Technology in a Postindustrial Age*. Cambridge: MIT Press, 1984.

Hirschman, Albert O. *The Passions and the Interests*. Princeton: Princeton University Press, 1977.

———. *The Rhetoric of Reaction: Perversity, Futility, Jeopardy*. Cambridge: Belknap, 1991.

Hockett, Robert C., and Saule T. Omarova. "The Finance Franchise." *Cornell Law Review* 102:5 (2017): 1143–1218.

Hodgson, Geoffrey M. *Conceptualizing Capitalism: Institutions, Evolution, Future*. Chicago: University of Chicago Press, 2015.

Hollingsworth, J. Rogers, and Robert Boyer, eds. *Contemporary Capitalism: The Embeddedness of Institutions*. Cambridge, U.K.: Cambridge University Press, 1997.

Jessop, Bob. "Knowledge as a Fictitious Commodity: Insights and Limits of a Polanyian Analysis." Pp. 115–134 in A. Bugra and K. Agartan, eds., *Reading Karl Polanyi for the 21st Century: Market Economy as a Political Project*. Basingstoke, U.K.: Palgrave, 2007.

———. "What Follows Neo-Liberalism? The Deepening Contradictions of US Domination and the Struggle for a New Global Order." Pp. 67–88 in Robert Albritton, Bob Jessop, and Richard Westra, eds., *Political Economy and Global Capitalism*. London: Anthem, 2010.

Jones, Daniel Stedman. *Masters of the Universe: Hayek, Friedman, and the Birth of Neoliberal Politics*. Princeton: Princeton University Press, 2012.

Judis, John. *The Populist Explosion: How the Great Recession Transformed American and European Politics*. New York: Columbia Global Reports, 2016.

Katznelson, Ira. *Fear Itself: The New Deal and the Origins of Our Time*. New York: Liveright, 2013.

Keck, Margaret, and Kathryn Sikkink. *Activists beyond Borders: Advocacy Networks in International Politics*. Ithaca: Cornell University Press, 1998.

Kennedy, Duncan. *A Critique of Adjudication (fin de siècle)*. Cambridge: Harvard University Press, 1997.

———. *Sexy Dressing, etc.: Essays on the Power and Politics of Cultural Identity*. Cambridge: Harvard University Press, 1993.

Kennedy, Paul. *The Rise and Fall of the Great Powers.* New York: Vintage Books, 1989.

Kenny, Charles. "Why Factory Jobs Are Shrinking Everywhere." *Bloomberg Business Week*, April 28, 2014. www.bloomberg.com/news/articles/2014–04–28/why-factory-jobs-are-shrinking-everywhere.

Kirkpatrick, L. Owen, and Michael P. Smith. "The Infrastructural Limits to Growth: Rethinking the Urban Growth Machine in Times of Fiscal Crisis." *International Journal of Urban and Regional Research* 35:3 (2011): 477–503.

Klare, Karl. "Critical Perspectives on Social and Economic Rights, Democracy, and Separation of Powers." Pp. 3–22 in Helena Alvisar Garcia, Karl Klare, and Lucy A. Williams, eds., *Social and Economic Rights in Theory and Practice.* New York: Routledge, 2015.

———. "Workplace Democracy and Market Reconstruction: An Agenda for Legal Reform." *Catholic University Law Review* 38:1 (1989): 3–68.

Klein, Naomi. *The Shock Doctrine: The Rise of Disaster Capitalism.* New York: Henry Holt, 2007.

Kloppenberg, James T. *Uncertain Victory: Social Democracy and Progressivism in European and American Thought, 1870–1920.* New York: Oxford University Press, 1986.

Knight, Will. "China Is Building a Robot Army of Model Workers." *Technology Review*, April 26, 2016. www.technologyreview.com/s/601215/china-is-building-a-robot-army-of-model-workers/.

Krippner, Greta. *Capitalizing on Crisis.* Cambridge: Harvard University Press, 2011.

Kristol, Irving. *Two Cheers for Capitalism.* New York: Basic Books, 1978.

Kwon, Hyeong-Ki. "Politics of Globalization and National Economy: The German Experience Compared with the United States." *Politics & Society* 40:4 (2012): 581–607.

Lazonick, William. "Profits without Prosperity." *Harvard Business Review*, September 2014.

———. *Sustainable Prosperity in the New Economy?* Kalamazoo, Mich.: Upjohn, 2009.

Lichtenstein, Nelson. *Labor's War at Home: The CIO in World War II.* New York: Cambridge University Press, 1982.

Lindblom, Charles. *Politics and Markets.* New York: Basic Books, 1977.

Lopez, Steven Henry. "Culture Change Management in Long-Term Care: A Shop-Floor View." *Politics & Society* 34:1 (2006): 55–80.

MacLean, Nancy. *Democracy in Chains: The Deep History of the Radical Right's Stealth Plan for America.* New York: Viking, 2017.

Madison, James. *Federalist Papers*, no. 10. http://avalon.law.yale.edu /18th_century/fed10.asp.

Mann, Michael. *The Sources of Social Power.* Vol. 1. Cambridge, U.K.: Cambridge University Press, 1986.

Matthijs, Matthias. "The Euro's 'Winner-Take-All' Political Economy: Institutional Choices, Policy Drift, and Diverging Patterns of Inequality." *Politics & Society* 44:3 (2016): 393–422.

Mayer, Jane. *Dark Money: The Hidden History of the Billionaires behind the Rise of the Radical Right.* New York: Doubleday, 2016.

McArthur, John B. "The Great Depression and the Limits of Market-Based Policy." PhD diss., School of Public Policy, University of California, Berkeley, 2003.

McLean, Bethany, and Joe Nocera. *All the Devils Are Here: The Hidden History of the Financial Crisis.* New York: Penguin, 2010.

Mills, C. Wright, *The Power Elite.* New York: Oxford University Press, 1956.

Mirowski, Philip, and Dieter Plehwe, eds. *The Road from Mont Pelerin.* Cambridge: Harvard University Press, 2009.

Morel, Nathalie, Bruno Palier, and Joakim Palme, eds. *Towards a Social Investment Welfare State? Ideas, Policies and Challenges.* Bristol: Policy Press, 2012.

Moreton, Bethany. *To Serve God and Wal-Mart.* Cambridge: Harvard University Press, 2009.

Nee, Victor, and Richard Swedberg, eds. *On Capitalism.* Stanford: Stanford University Press, 2007.

Nelson, Moira, and John D. Stephens. "Do Social Investment Policies Produce More and Better Jobs?" Pp. 205–234 in Nathalie Morel, Bruno Palier, and Joakim Palme, eds., *Towards a Social Investment Welfare State?* Bristol: Policy Press, 2012.

Newfield, Christopher. *Unmaking the Public University: The Forty-Year Assault on the Middle Class*. Cambridge: Harvard University Press, 2008.

Norton, Michael I., and Dan Ariely. "Building a Better America— One Wealth Quintile at a Time." *Perspectives on Psychological Science* 6:1 (2011): 9–12.

Page, Benjamin I., and Larry Jacobs. *Class War? What Americans Really Think about Economic Inequality.* Chicago: University of Chicago Press, 2009.

Parijs, Phillipe Van, and Yannick Vanderborght. *Basic Income: A Radical Proposal for a Free Society and a Sane Economy.* Cambridge: Harvard University Press, 2017.

Peck, Jamie, and Nik Theodore. "Variegated Capitalism." *Progress in Human Geography* 31:6 (2007): 731–772.

Phillips-Fein, Kim. *Invisible Hands: The Businessmen's Crusade against the New Deal.* New York: Norton, 2009.

Piketty, Thomas. *Capital in the Twenty-First Century.* Trans. Arthur Goldhammer. Cambridge: Harvard University Press, 2014.

Piven, Frances Fox. *Challenging Authority: How Ordinary People Change America.* Lanham, Md.: Rowman and Littlefield.

Platt, Eric. "Corporates Lead Surge to Record $6.6 Trillion Debt Issuance." *Financial Times,* December 27, 2016. www.ft.com/content/e3f0e766-cc46-11e6-b8ce-b9c03770f8b1.

Polanyi, Karl. *The Great Transformation: The Political and Economic Origins of Our Time.* Boston: Beacon Press, 2001 [1944].

Pontusson, Jonas. *Inequality and Prosperity: Social Europe vs. Liberal America.* Ithaca: Cornell University Press, 2006.

Prasad, Monica. *The Land of Too Much: American Abundance and the Paradox of Poverty.* Cambridge: Harvard University Press, 2012.

Rand, Ayn. *Capitalism: The Unknown Ideal.* New York: New American Library, 1966.

Reddaway, Peter, and Dmitri Glinski. *The Tragedy of Russia's Reforms: Market Bolshevism against Democracy.* Washington, D.C.: U.S. Institute of Peace Press, 2001.

Riesman, David, Nathan Glazer, and Ruell Denney. *The Lonely Crowd: A Study of the Changing American Character.* New Haven: Yale University Press, 1950.

Robertson, Charles J. *Temple of Invention: History of a National Landmark.* London: Scala, 2006.

Rodgers, Daniel T. *Atlantic Crossings: Social Politics in a Progressive Age.* Cambridge: Belknap, 1998.

Ruggie, John. "International Regimes, Transactions, and Change: Embedded Liberalism in the Postwar Economic Order." *International Organization* 36:2 (1982): 372–415.

Sahlins, Marshall. *Culture and Practical Reason*. Chicago: University of Chicago Press, 1976.

Sandbrook, Richard. *Reinventing the Left in the Global South: The Politics of the Possible*. Cambridge, U.K.: Cambridge University Press, 2014.

Skidelsky, Robert. *John Maynard Keynes*. Vol. 3, *Fighting for Freedom, 1937–1946*. New York: Penguin, 2001.

Sklar, Martin J. *The United States as a Developing Country: Studies in U.S. History in the Progressive Era and the 1920s*. New York: Cambridge University Press, 1992.

Skocpol, Theda, and Alexander Hertel-Fernandez. "The Koch Network and Republican Party Extremism." *Perspectives on Politics* 14:3 (2016): 681–699.

Skocpol, Theda, and Vanessa Williamson. *The Tea Party and the Remaking of Republican Conservatism*. New York: Oxford University Press, 2012.

Smith, Adam. *The Theory of Moral Sentiments*. Cambridge, U.K.: Cambridge University Press, 2002 [1759].

———. *The Wealth of Nations*. Chicago: University of Chicago Press, 1976 [1776].

Soltes, Eugene. *Why They Do It: Inside the Mind of the White-Collar Criminal*. New York: Public Affairs, 2016.

Somers, Margaret. *Genealogies of Citizenship: Markets, Statelessness, and the Right to Have Rights*. New York: Cambridge University Press, 2008.

Speidel, Richard E. "The 'Duty' of Good Faith in Contract Performance and Enforcement." *Journal of Legal Education* 46:4 (1996): 537–545.

Stiglitz, Joseph. *Rewriting the Rules of the American Economy: An Agenda for Growth and Shared Prosperity*. New York: Norton, 2016.

———. *Whither Socialism?* Cambridge: MIT Press, 1994.

Stiglitz , Joseph, Amartya Sen, and Jean-Paul Fitoussi. *Mis-measuring Our Lives: Why GDP Doesn't Add Up*. New York: New Press, 2010.

Streeck, Wolfgang. *Buying Time: The Delayed Crisis of Democratic Capitalism*. Trans. Patrick Camiller. London: Verso, 2014.

———. *How Will Capitalism End? Essays on a Failing System*. London: Verso, 2016.

———. *Re-forming Capitalism: Institutional Change in the German Political Economy*. New York: Oxford University Press, 2009.

Swedberg, Richard. *The Max Weber Dictionary: Key Words and Central Concepts*. Stanford: Stanford University Press, 2005.

Teles, Stephen M. *The Rise of the Conservative Legal Movement: The Battle for Control of the Law.* Princeton: Princeton University Press, 2009.

Thelen, Kathleen. *How Institutions Evolve: The Political Economy of Skills in Germany, Britain, the United States and Japan.* New York: Cambridge University Press, 2004.

Tocqueville, Alexis de. *Democracy in America.* 2 vols. Trans. Henry Reeve. New York: Vintage Books, 1945 [1835, 1840].

TyreeHageman, Jennifer. "From Silicon Valley to Wall Street: Following the Rise of an Entrepreneurial Ethos." *Berkeley Journal of Sociology* 57 (2013): 74–113.

Unger, Roberto Mangabeira. *False Necessity: Anti-Necessitarian Social Theory in the Service of Radical Democracy.* Part 1 of *Politics: A Work in Constructive Social Theory.* New York: Cambridge University Press, 1987.

United Nations Conference on Trade and Development. *World Investment Report 2015: Reforming International Investment Governance.* New York: United Nations, 2015.

Useem, Michael. *Executive Defense: Shareholder Power and Corporate Reorganization.* Cambridge: Harvard University Press, 1993.

Varoufakis, Yanis. *And the Weak Suffer What They Must? Europe's Crisis and America's Economic Future.* New York: Nation Books, 2016.

Volkov, Vadim. "Between Economy and the State: Private Security and Rule Enforcement in Russia." *Politics & Society* 28:4 (2000): 483–501.

Wallerstein, Immanuel. *The Essential Wallerstein.* New York: New Press, 2000.

———. *The Modern World-System: Capitalist Agriculture and the Origins of the European World-Economy in the Sixteenth Century.* New York: Academic Press, 1977.

Weber, Max. *The Protestant Ethic and the Spirit of Capitalism.* Trans. Talcott Parsons. Los Angeles: Roxbury, 1998 [1904–1905].

Weiss, Linda, and Elizabeth Thurbon. "The Business of Buying American: Public Procurement as Trade Strategy in the USA." *Review of International Political Economy* 13:5 (2006): 701–724.

Winters, Jeffrey. *Oligarchy.* New York: Cambridge University Press, 2011.

Wood, Ellen Meiksins. *The Origin of Capitalism: A Longer View.* London: Verso, 2002.

Woodruff, David. *Money Unmade: Barter and the Fate of Russian Capitalism.* Ithaca: Cornell University Press, 1999.

Wright, Gavin. *Sharing the Prize: The Economics of the Civil Rights Revolution in the American South*. Cambridge: Belknap, 2013.

Zelizer, Viviana. "How I Became a Relational Economic Sociologist and What That Means." *Politics & Society* 40:2 (2012): 145–174.

———. *The Purchase of Intimacy*. Princeton: Princeton University Press, 2005.

Zysman, John. *Governments, Markets, and Growth*. Ithaca: Cornell University Press, 1983.

Index

abolitionist movement, 77

activists/activism: for civil rights, 78, 117; and complacency, 182; and global order, 169–70, 172–73, 174; right-wing, 34, 67; use of "capitalism by," 202. *See also* social movements

"adventurers' capitalism," 92

advertising, 93, 94

agnosticism in reform, 211–12

agriculture, 45–46, *46 fig 1,* 48–50, 130

anti-immigrant political parties, 181

anti-trust enforcement, 200

Asian Infrastructure Bank, 170–71, 196

austerity measures: and electoral revolt, 5; and "Eurosclerosis," 81–82; and global order, 149, 150, 163, 166–67, 171; in glut of saving, 189–90; in slow growth, 180–82

autocracies, 64–65, 70, 212

automation, 138–39, 140

automobile manufacturing, 47, 136–37, 186–87

autonomy: and capitalist illusion, 10–11; and democracy, 60–61; and global economy, 29; of market economies, 32–39, 112, 178–79; in perversity thesis, 176–77; in social theory, 29

bancor currency plan, 194–95, 197

bankers, 7, 97–98. *See also* financial sector

banks, 8, 40, 41, 61–62, 167–68, 193–94, 195–96, 197

bargaining power, 31, 149, 162

Bell, Daniel, 25; *The Cultural Contradictions of Capitalism,* 93

Bernanke, Ben, 193

bilingualism, 93–94, 96, 114

biological essentialism, 120–21, 144

biology analogy for system change, 117–18

Bobos in Paradise (Brooks), 99